28 Mock Tests
for
Olympiad
CLASS 4

Science | Mathematics | English
Logical Reasoning | GK | Cyber

DISHA™
Publication Inc

In the interest of student community
Circulation of softcopy of Book(s) in pdf or other equivalent format(s) through any social media channels, emails, etc. or any other channels through mobiles, laptops or desktops is a criminal offence. Anybody circulating, downloading, storing, softcopy of the Book on his device(s) is in breach of the Copyright Act. Further Photocopying of this book or any of its material is also illegal. Do not download or forward in case you come across any such softcopy material.

DISHA Publications Inc.

45, 2nd Floor, Maharishi Dayanand Marg,
Corner Market, Malviya Nagar, new Delhi -110017
Tel: 49842349/ 49842350

© Copyright DISHA Publication Inc.

All Rights Reserved. No part of this publication may be reproduced in any form without prior permission of the publisher. The author and the publisher do not take any legal responsibility for any errors or misrepresentations that might have crept in.
We have tried and made our best efforts to provide accurate up-to-date information in this book.

Typeset By

DISHA DTP Team

Buying books from DISHA

Just Got A Lot More Rewarding!!!

We at DISHA Publication, value your feedback immensely and to show our appercipation of our reviewers, we have launched a review contest.

To participate in this reward scheme, just follow these quick and simple steps:
- Write a review of the product you purchase on Amazon/Flipkart.
- Take a screenshot/photo of your review.
- Mail it to *disha-rewards@aiets.co.in*, along with all your details.

Each month, selected reviewers will win exciting gifts from DISHA Publication. Note that the rewards for each month will be declared in the first week of next month on our website.

https://bit.ly/review-reward-disha.

Write To
Us At

feedback_disha@aiets.co.in

CONTENTS

English

1. Mock Test 1 — E-1-7
2. Mock Test 2 — E-8-12
3. Mock Test 3 — E-13-17
4. Mock Test 4 — E-18-22
5. Mock Test 5 — E-23-30

Mathematics

1. Mock Test 1 — M-1-8
2. Mock Test 2 — M-9-16
3. Mock Test 3 — M-17-23
4. Mock Test 4 — M-24-34
5. Mock Test 5 — M-35-40

Science

1. Mock Test 1 — S-1-7
2. Mock Test 2 — S-8-14
3. Mock Test 3 — S-15-20
4. Mock Test 4 — S-21-26
5. Mock Test 5 — S-27-32

General Knowledge

1. Mock Test 1 — G-1-5
2. Mock Test 2 — G-6-10
3. Mock Test 3 — G-11-14
4. Mock Test 4 — G-15-22
5. Mock Test 5 — G-23-30

Logical Reasoning

1. Mock Test 1 — L$_R$-1-6
2. Mock Test 2 — L$_R$-7-12
3. Mock Test 3 — L$_R$-13-17
4. Mock Test 4 — L$_R$-18-22
5. Mock Test 5 — L$_R$-23-28

Cyber

1. Mock Test 1 — c-1-6
2. Mock Test 2 — c-7-13
3. Mock Test 3 — c-14-20

Hints and Explanations — 1-54

Unlock your child's HIDDEN GENIUS! with Olympiad Champs

Scan code to gain **FREE access** to **"Olympiad Champs"**, a unique page dedicated to prepare students of class 1-8 to ace all National Level Olympiad Exams.

Current Affairs Updates, Mock Tests, Past Papers, Quizzes, Interesting, Fun Facts, Parenting Articles & Free Courses

ENGLISH MOCK TEST 1-5

OLYMPIAD Mock Test 1

Name : _____
Number of Questions : 35
Max. Marks : 35
Time : 1 Hour 30 Minutes

There is no negative marking in the test.

DIRECTIONS (Qs. 1 to 3): For the following sentences, select which kind of noun the underlined word is.

1. <u>Ram</u> is going to the market.
   (a) Proper noun
   (b) Common noun
   (c) Collective noun
   (d) Abstract noun

2. Sita went to the garden and saw a <u>flock of birds</u>.
   (a) Proper noun
   (b) Common noun
   (c) Collective noun
   (d) Abstract noun

3. The women went to see the <u>butterflies</u>.
   (a) Proper noun
   (b) Common noun
   (c) Collective noun
   (d) Abstract noun

DIRECTION (Qs. 4): Tick the appropriate verb (use of 'being' verbs).

4. Last year they _____ too young to go by themselves.
   (a) is   (b) am
   (c) was   (d) were

DIRECTIONS (Qs. 5 & 6): Fill the blanks with suitable pronouns.

5. Jolly is a pretty girl. _____ has long hair.
   (a) He   (b) They
   (c) It   (d) She

Space for Rough Work

6. Mandy is crying. Those toys that broke are _____.
   (a) theirs   (b) his
   (c) hers   (d) ours

DIRECTIONS (Qs. 7 & 8): Select the adjectives in the following sentences.

7. Kohinoor is the world's biggest diamond.
   (a) Kohinoor   (b) Is
   (c) World's   (d) Biggest

8. Manohar loves red roses.
   (a) Manohar   (b) Loves
   (c) Red   (d) Roses

DIRECTIONS (Qs. 9 & 10): Select the adverbs in the following sentences.

9. Mr. Rochester wants to meet the ladies tonight.
   (a) Wants   (b) To meet
   (c) Ladies   (d) Tonight

10. He fell asleep and slept soundly.
    (a) He   (b) Slept
    (c) Soundly   (d) Asleep

DIRECTION (Qs. 11): Fill in the correct prepositions in the blanks.

11. I received a letter _____ my grandma.
    (a) from   (b) soon
    (c) at   (d) with

DIRECTIONS (Qs. 12 & 13): Fill in the blanks using conjunctions (and/but/so/because).

12. My name is Jim _____ I'm your new teacher.
    (a) and   (b) but
    (c) so   (d) because

13. We'll have to go shopping _____ we have nothing for dinner.
    (a) and   (b) but
    (c) so   (d) because

DIRECTIONS (Qs. 14 & 15): Choose the correct form of verb according to the tense specified in the brackets.

14. The doctor _____ the patient. (Present Tense)
    (a) treat   (b) treats
    (c) treated   (d) will treat

15. Sheela _____ a white dog. (Simple Past Tense)

    (a) buys (b) bought
    (c) will buy (d) buying

DIRECTION (Qs. 16): Select the correct article.

16. She is _____ attractive girl.

    (a) a (b) an
    (c) the (d) nothing

DIRECTIONS (Qs. 17 & 18): Select the synonym of the words given below.

17. Wealthy

    (a) Poor (b) Hungry
    (c) Miserable (d) Rich

18. Middle

    (a) Corner (b) Centre
    (c) End (d) Beginning

DIRECTIONS (Qs. 19 & 20): Select the antonyms of the words given below.

19. Attack

    (a) Defend (b) Damage
    (c) Hurt (d) Harm

20. Blunt

    (a) Dull (b) Rounded
    (c) Honest (d) Sharp

21. The shopkeeper showed me a range of pens. He showed me pens of every type and colour, from the cheapest to the most expensive. He showed me ball pens, ink pens, gel pens and many more. In the sentence above, "range" means "_____".

    (a) wide variety
    (b) large size
    (c) beautiful set
    (d) good quality

22. Choose the word with the correct spelling for the sentence below. I was so sleepy that I fell asleep at the _____ table.

    (a) dineing (b) dinning
    (c) dining (d) diening

23. Today I was late for school. But since it had happened for the first time, the teacher did not punish me. Which word can replace "did not punish" in the sentence given above?

    (a) Excused (b) Explained
    (c) Examined (d) Expected

24. Imagine yor are Samir. It is your birthday next week and you are hosting a party for your friends at your home in the evening at 6.30.

Complete the following invitation to Vikas with choices given below:

13th August 2017

12 Green Park

Sadhna Enclave,

New Delhi-110004

Dear Vikas,

It is my birthday on Sunday, 20th August. I am giving a party to my friends. I am organising many games. My didi is planning to _____ our favorite dishes. It will be fun time for all the friends. Please do join us at 6.30 p.m. at my house.

Samir

(a) eat (b) cook
(c) drink (d) none of these

DIRECTIONS (Qs. 25 & 26): From the following options given, select the one which is correct.

25. (a) ali invited suresh and anil on his birthday party.
 (b) Ali invited suresh and anil on his birthday party
 (c) Ali invited Suresh and Anil on his birthday party.
 (d) ali invited Suresh and Anil on his birthday party.

26. (a) What is your full name ?
 (b) what is your full name ?
 (c) What is your full name.
 (d) what is your full name.

DIRECTIONS (Qs. 27 to 29): Read the passage and answer the following questions.

PASSAGE

India is an ancient country. Many great kings have ruled over India. Some of them built wonderful buildings that today remind us of them. The most famous of these is the Taj Mahal at Agra.

The Mughal kings built many buildings. One of the greatest Mughals was Emperor Shah Jahan. He was known to be fond of large and beautiful buildings. Shah Jahan loved his wife Arjumand Bano Begum very much. In fact, he changed her name to Mumtaz Mahal. When she died, the emperor was very sad. He wanted something which would remind him of her and her beauty.

Shah Jahan decided to build a marvelous tomb for her. This tomb was to be no ordinary grave. It was to be the Taj Mahal, a grand monument in memory of a beloved empress. It took twenty-two years to build. Hundreds of workers toiled at the task of getting it ready. The best materials were brought from all over. It cost about three crores to build. Shah Jahan left no stone unturned in planning and building the tomb. He wanted the world to see and wonder at the beauty of the Taj Mahal.

The Taj Mahal is built of white marble that shines with different hues at different times of the day. This magnificent structure looks beautiful especially on a full moon night. Thousands of tourists from India and abroad come to visit the Taj each year. On a particular full moon night in October, there are a very large number of tourists. This is the night when the Taj looks more beautiful than on any other night. Indians are proud of this monument.

27. Taj Mahal is located at
    (a) Agra   (b) Mumbai
    (c) New Delhi (d) Jaipur

28. Who built the Taj ?
    (a) Akbar
    (b) Ashoka, the great
    (c) Shah Jahan
    (d) Humayun

29. How long did it take to build the Taj ?
    (a) 5 years   (b) 22 years
    (c) 34 years   (d) 10 years

DIRECTIONS (Qs. 30 to 32): Read the poem given below and answer the questions that follow.

Freedom is the right to do
Anything that pleases you,
As long as you keep in sight
That others also have a right,
Have you the right to kill a cat?
Oh no! It's wrong, just consider that
The cat has the right to live like you

A right to eating and drinking too!
So remember that it's certainly wrong
To deprive a nightingale its song
To cheat the poor people, as rich men do
To rob the innocent, as robbers do
To insure someone to win a race
To despise some and others embrace
To disobey every order and rule
And drown a swimmer in the pool
And shout and scream like a fool
Disrespecting the teachers in the school.
So never forget that although you are free,
You should think of
others, not only 'ME'.

30. What are the rights of a cat similar to ours?

(a) The right to live
(b) The right to eat
(c) The right to drink
(d) All of the above

31. What similarity has the poet pointed out between rich men and robbers?

(a) They rob the innocent
(b) They hide from the police
(c) They give alms to the poor
(d) None of the above

32. How should students conduct themselves in the school?

(a) They should shout and scream and disrespect the teachers.
(b) They should not shout and scream and disrespect the teachers.
(c) They should rob the innocent.
(d) They should scold younger students.

DIRECTIONS (Qs. 33 to 35): Read the story given below and answer the following questions.

PASSAGE

Ruskin Bond (from The Hare in the Moon)

A long time ago, when animals could talk, there lived in a forest four wise creatures - a hare, a jackal, an otter and a monkey.

They were good friends, and every evening they would sit together in a forest glade to discuss the events of the day, exchange advice and make good resolutions. The hare was the noblest and wisest of the four. He believed in the superiority of men and women, and was always telling his friends tales of human goodness and wisdom.

———————————— *Space for Rough Work* ————————————

One evening, when the moon rose in the sky and those days the moon's face was clear and unmarked, the hare looked up at it carefully and said, "Tomorrow good men will observe a fast, for I can see that it will be the middle of the month. They will eat no food before sunset, and during the day they will give alms to any beggar to holy man who may meet them. Let us promise to do the same. In that way, we can come a little closer to human beings in dignity and respect."

The others agreed, and then went their different ways.

Next day, the otter got up, stretched himself, and was preparing to get his breakfast when he remembered the vow he had taken with his friends.

"If I keep my word, how hungry I shall be by evening!" he thought." I'd better make sure that there's plenty to eat once the fast is over." He set off towards the river.

A fisherman had caught several large fish early that morning, and had buried them in the sand, planning to return for them later. The otter soon smelt them out.

"A supper all ready for me," he said to himself. "But since it's holy day, I mustn't steal." Instead he called out, "Does anyone own this fish?"

There being no answer, the otter carried the fish off to his home, setting it aside for his evening meat.

33. How many wise animals lived in the forest?
    (a) 4   (b) 2
    (c) 3   (d) 5

34. Every evening the four friends,
    (a) discussed the events of the day, exchanged advice and made good resolutions.
    (b) went hunting for food and shared their meals.
    (c) sat around a campfire and shared old stories.
    (d) none of the above

35. What noble deed was usually performed on the day of the fast?
    (a) Give alms to beggars or a holy man.
    (b) Sing prayers.
    (c) Give sweets to children.
    (d) All of the above

OLYMPIAD Mock Test 2

Name : _____   Max. Marks : 35
Number of Questions : 35   Time : 1 Hour 30 Minutes

There is no negative marking in the test.

1. Living things usually live and move together in groups. Tick the correct animal corresponding to the group.
   A shoal of
   (a) Monkeys   (b) Fish
   (c) Lions   (d) Tigers

2. What is the prefix in disassociate?
   (a) ate   (b) dis
   (c) sociate   (d) as

DIRECTION (Q. 3): Tick the appropriate verb (use of 'being' verbs).

3. Hansel and Gretel ____ characters in a fairytale.
   (a) is   (b) are
   (c) am   (d) was

DIRECTIONS (Qs. 4 to 6): Fill the blanks with suitable pronoun.

4. The cruel farmer hit ____ ox so badly that it fell down.
   (a) their   (b) hers
   (c) his   (d) theirs

5. ____ went for a long walk in the park.
   (a) Them   (b) Theirs
   (c) Ours   (d) We

6. The teacher gave ____ a surprise treat for being good children.
   (a) us   (b) her
   (c) him   (d) it

———— Space for Rough Work ————

7. Please _____ your essay by wednesday afternoon.
   (a) hand in   (b) hand over
   (c) hand on   (d) hand out

DIRECTION (Qs. 8): Select adjectives from the following sentences.

8. Manish went to the garden to hear the black bird sing beautifully.
   (a) Garden   (b) To hear
   (c) Black   (d) Beautifully

DIRECTIONS (Qs. 9 & 10): Select the adverbs in the following sentences.

9. Once there was very good and brave Japanese man named Hidesato.
   (a) Once   (b) Man
   (c) Brave   (d) Named

10. A week _____ has seven days.
    (a) always   (b) never
    (c) sometimes (d) rarely

DIRECTIONS (Qs. 11 & 12): Fill in the correct prepositions in the blanks.

11. I got up _____ six o' clock.
    (a) at   (b) in
    (c) into   (d) on

12. I drove a car _____ the morning.
    (a) up   (b) on
    (c) in   (d) onto

DIRECTIONS (Qs. 13 to 15): Fill in the blanks using conjunctions (and/but/so/because).

13. The history test was difficult _____ the English one was easy.
    (a) and   (b) but
    (c) so   (d) because

14. We didn't go to the beach yesterday _____ it was raining.
    (a) and   (b) but
    (c) so   (d) because

15. We have a test on Monday _____ I'll have to study this weekend.
    (a) and   (b) but
    (c) so   (d) because

――――――― Space for Rough Work ―――――――

DIRECTION (Qs. 16): Choose the correct form of verb according to the tense specified in the brackets.

16. Mr. Sharma _____ a red car. (Present Tense)
    (a) owns   (b) will own
    (c) owned   (d) own

DIRECTIONS (Qs. 17 & 18): Select the correct article.

17. Alice drives ___ old car that belonged to her uncle.
    (a) a   (b) an
    (c) the   (d) nothing

18. Do you have _____ computer?
    (a) a   (b) an
    (c) the   (d) nothing

DIRECTIONS (Qs. 19 & 20): Select the synonym of the words given below.

19. Accurate
    (a) Correct   (b) Incorrect
    (c) Wrong   (d) Possible

20. Admire
    (a) Praise   (b) Allow
    (c) Obey   (d) Play

DIRECTIONS (Qs. 21 to 23): Select the antonym of the words given below.

21. Expensive
    (a) Costly   (b) Dear
    (c) Cheap   (d) Steep

22. Famous
    (a) Unknown   (b) Well-known
    (c) Eminent   (d) Infamous

23. Deep
    (a) Shallow   (b) Open
    (c) Tall   (d) Long

24. What change in capitalization should be made to the sentence below?

    The author t.s. Eliot wrote a poem about a man Alfred Prufrock who walked the streets of London.

    (a) change author to Author
    (b) change t.s. to T.S.
    (c) change poem to Poem
    (d) change Alfred to alfred

25. Which possessive noun completes the sentence?

    The jacket belongs to the man. It is the _____ jacket.

    (a) man's (b) mans'
    (c) mans   (d) men's

26. Choose the correct phrase to finish the sentence.

    Melissa keeps quiet when she is _____.

    (a) at the park (b) in the library
    (c) on the boat (d) in the party

27. Choose the correct word to fill in the blank.

    I have six _____.

    (a) pencils' (b) pencil's
    (c) pencils   (d) pencil

28. What is the punctuation mark in the word school's?

    (a) comma   (b) semi-colon
    (c) hyphen (d) apostrophe

DIRECTION (Qs. 29): From the following options given, select the one which is correct.

29. (a) can! you speak English?
    (b) can you speak english
    (c) Can you speak English?
    (d) can you speak English

DIRECTIONS (Qs. 30 to 32): Read the passages and answer the following questions.

PASSAGE

Coconut oil is used in India as cooking oil, hair oil, body oil and industrial oil. It accounts for 6 percent of the total vegetable oil pool in the country.

Coconut oil becomes colourless to pale brownish yellow. It is extracted from dried coconut kernel. The oil is fluid as water under warm conditions but solidifies at cooler temperatures. It is neutral in its effects on blood, fats and cholesterol. It is also an excellent hair oil. It prevents dandruff and keeps the

Space for Rough Work

skin soft and moist. In addition, the oil is extensively used in ice-creams, whipped cream, biscuits and similar products.

30. Coconut oil is used in India as
(a) hair oil (b) cooking oil
(c) body oil (d) all of these

31. Coconut oil is extracted from
(a) dried coconut kernel
(b) bark of coconut tree
(c) coconut tree leaves
(d) coconut water

32. Coconut oil is _____ at warm temperature but solidifies at _____ temperature.
(a) fluid, warm (b) solid, cool
(c) fluid, cool (d) solid, warm

DIRECTIONS (Qs. 33 to 35): Read the poem given below and answer the questions that follow.

Where the pools are bright and deep
Where the grey trout lies asleep;
Up the river and o'er the lea,
That's the way for Billy and me.
Where the blackbird signs the latest,
Where the hawthorn blooms the sweetest
Where the nestlings chirp and flee,
That's the way for Billy and me.
Where the mower's mow the cleanest,
Where the hay lies thick and greenest,
There to track the homeward bee,
That's the way for Billy and me.
Where the hazel bank is steepest
Where the shadow falls the deepest,
Where the clustering nuts fall free,
That's the way for Billy and me.

Write the words from the poem which describe the given words:

33. The pool is described as
(a) bright and deep
(b) shallow and steep
(c) dirty and green
(d) blue and deep

34. The hay is
(a) thick and brown
(b) thick and green
(c) grey and yellow
(d) thin and green

35. The trout is
(a) grey and awake
(b) blue and awake
(c) grey and asleep
(d) blue and asleep

Space for Rough Work

OLYMPIAD Mock Test 3

Name: _____
Number of Questions : 35

Max. Marks : 35
Time : 1 Hour 30 Minutes

There is no negative marking in the test.

DIRECTIONS (Qs. 1 to 4): Choose the correct part of speech of the underlined words.

1. <u>Zacob's</u> bike is old.
   (a) Proper noun
   (b) Common noun
   (c) Collective noun
   (d) Material noun

2. The <u>doctor</u> is checking patients
   (a) Proper noun
   (b) Collective noun
   (c) Common noun
   (d) Material noun

3. <u>That</u> is a bat.
   (a) Reflexive Pronoun
   (b) Personal Pronoun
   (c) Interrogative Pronoun
   (d) Demonstrative Pronoun

4. <u>Who</u> did this work ?
   (a) Reflexive Pronoun
   (b) Demonstrative Pronoun
   (c) Interrogative Pronoun
   (d) Possessive Pronoun

5. What is the present continuous form (V4) of shine ?
   (a) Shining   (b) Shone
   (c) Shines   (d) Shones

6. Identify the negative words in the sentence.
   I have no choice but to go.
   (a) go   (b) have
   (c) no   (d) choice

7. Which word uses un- in the same way as in the word unhappy?
   (a) under   (b) unite
   (c) unicorn   (d) unsafe

———————— Space for Rough Work ————————

8. There is _____ awesome game in that place.

   Which word is an article and best completes the sentence?

   (a) a (b) an
   (c) many (d) crazy

DIRECTIONS (Qs. 9 to 13) : Fill in the correct preposition.

9. Who is _____ the room?
   (a) to (b) from
   (c) for (d) inside

10. January comes _____ February.
    (a) to (b) with
    (c) before (d) under

11. He earns money _____ teaching the children.
    (a) by (b) for
    (c) from (d) with

12. He cannot run _____ he is injured.
    (a) though (b) because
    (c) with (d) so

13. He was punished _____ he was not guilty.
    (a) though (b) but
    (c) as (d) so

14. What is the past form (V2) of sleep ?
    (a) Sleeps (b) Slept
    (c) Sleeping (d) Sleep

15. What is the Past Participle form (V3) of Eat ?
    (a) Eat (b) Eats
    (c) Ate (d) Eaten

DIRECTIONS (Qs. 16 & 17) : Fill in the correct article.

16. Everybody respects Sanjay as he is _____ honorable person.
    (a) a (b) an
    (c) the (d) none of these

17. _____ Himalayas is one of the youngest mountains in the world.
    (a) A (b) An
    (c) The (d) None of these

DIRECTIONS (Qs. 18 & 19): Choose the correct form of verb.

18. I have not _____ him today. (see)
    (a) seen (b) sea
    (c) saw (d) sees

Space for Rough Work

Mock Test-3

19. I have _____ to him yesterday. (talk)
    (a) talks   (b) talked
    (c) talking   (d) talkative

20. Which word uses -ly in the same way as in the word nicely?
    (a) sly   (b) fondly
    (c) family   (d) tally

21. Identify the option with correct spelling to complete the sentence given below. The_____took his sheep and goats to graze on the mountains.
    (a) shepard   (b) shepherd
    (c) shepperd   (d) sheepherd

22. Shahrukh Khan is a *"famous"* actor today. But when he came to Mumbai several years ago, he was almost _____. Which word is opposite in meaning to "famous" and can be used to complete the sentence given above?
    (a) poor   (b) unknown
    (c) familiar   (d) worthless

DIRECTIONS (Qs. 23 & 24): Choose the correct word/phrase to complete each sentence.

23. There were too many people at the party and there wasn't _____ food for everyone.
    (a) too much   (b) many
    (c) some   (d) enough

24. Saleem is a _____ swimmer than Kapil.
    (a) better   (b) good
    (c) best   (d) slowest

25. Select the phrase/word to match the description.
    You can pour this; it has no fixed shape and takes the shape of its container. It's_____.
    (a) flexible
    (b) fluid
    (c) stretchable
    (d) stiff

Space for Rough Work

26. Choose the best reply to complete each conversation.

Babu : Hey, it's New Years Eve, why aren't you dancing? Let's dance.

Rinku : I'm not _____.

(a) at a dancing party

(b) a moody dancer

(c) in a dancing mood

(d) at my party

DIRECTIONS (Qs. 27 to 29): Read the following paragraph and answer the questions.

Modern-day Easter is derived from two traditions : one Judeo-Christian and other Pagan. Both Christians and Pagans have celebrated death and resurrection themes following the Spring Equinox for millennia. Most religious historians believe that many elements of the Christian observation of Easter were derived from earlier Pagan celebrations. The equinox occurs each year on March 20, 21, or 22. Both Neo-pagans and Christians continue to celebrate religious rituals linked to the equinox. Wiccans and other Neopagans usually hold their celebrations on the day or eve of the equinox. Western Christians celebrate Easter on the Sunday on or after the full moon that follows the nominal date of the Equinox — Mar-21. The Eastern Orthodox churches follow a different calculation; their Easter celebration is often many weeks after the date selected by the Western churches.

27. In which of the following religions Easter is celebrated ?

(a) Hinduism

(b) Parsee

(c) Christianity

(d) Jewish

28. What is the belief of religious historians about Easter ?

(a) Elements of Easter were derived form earlier Pagan celebrations.

(b) Pagan celebrations is part and parcel of Easter.

(c) Elements of Easter were derived from Judeo - Christian.

(d) All of these

Space for Rough Work

29. When do western Christians celebrate Easter?
    (a) On the Sunday
    (b) On the Sunday on or after the full moon that follows the nominal date of the Equinox - MAR - 21
    (c) After the full moon that follows the nominal date of the Equinox MAR-21
    (d) All of these

DIRECTIONS (Qs. 30 to 33): Choose the type of noun of the underline word.

30. He has good <u>knowledge</u> of English.
    (a) Proper noun
    (b) Common noun
    (c) Collective noun
    (d) Abstract noun

31. He <u>himself</u> told me about this matter.
    (a) Reflexive pronoun
    (b) Emphasizing pronoun
    (c) Demonstrative pronoun
    (d) Interrogative pronoun

32. <u>Whom</u> do you praise?
    (a) Interrogative pronoun
    (b) Demonstrative pronoun
    (c) Possessive pronoun
    (d) Personal pronoun

33. People pray to God at different <u>places</u>.
    (a) Collective noun
    (b) Common noun
    (c) Proper noun
    (d) Material noun

34. Which words correctly complete this sentence?

    ____ honest complaint is better than ____ false compliment.
    (a) A . . . a   (b) An . . . an
    (c) An . . . a   (d) A . . . an

35. What is the correct possessive form of the phrase?
    Swim team for boys
    (a) boys swim team
    (b) boy's swim team
    (c) boys' swim team
    (d) boys's swim team

OLYMPIAD Mock Test 4

Name : _____
Number of Questions : 40
Max. Marks : 40
Time : 2 Hours

There is no negative marking in the test.

DIRECTIONS (Qs. 1 to 3): Choose the correct part of the speech of the underlined word.

1. He is fond of <u>wine</u>.
   (a) Common noun
   (b) Material noun
   (c) Proper noun
   (d) Collective noun

2. The <u>bird</u> is flying.
   (a) Proper noun
   (b) Collective noun
   (c) Material noun
   (d) Common noun

3. She has lost her <u>bunch of keys</u>.
   (a) Proper noun
   (b) Common noun
   (c) Material noun
   (d) Collective noun

4. What is the past tense form (V2) of shine ?
   (a) Shine   (b) Shone
   (c) Shining   (d) Shined

5. The first match will take place _____ India and Pakistan.
   (a) between   (b) among
   (c) to   (d) for

6. She will reach there _____ Monday.
   (a) at   (b) on
   (c) to   (d) in

7. I told you _____ he will not dance.
   (a) though   (b) but
   (c) as   (d) that

8. What is the past tense (V2) of grow ?
   (a) Grow   (b) Grow
   (c) Grew   (d) Growing

―――――― *Space for Rough Work* ――――――

9. What is the Past Particle form (V3) of take ?
   (a) Tooks   (b) Took
   (c) Take   (d) Taken

10. The woman found _____ one rupee coin on the road.
    (a) an   (b) the
    (c) a   (d) none of these

11. He _____ me yesterday. (meet)
    (a) met   (b) meet
    (c) meets   (d) meeting

12. Titanic _____ in the ocean. (sink)
    (a) sank   (b) sinks
    (c) sunk   (d) sinking

13. She _____ watching TV for 15 minutes. (watch)
    (a) has watching
    (b) have watched
    (c) has been watching
    (d) all of these

14. Choose the best form of LOUD to complete the sentence.
    Amber is the _____ girl in the choir. (superlative)
    (a) loudest   (b) louder
    (c) loud   (d) more loud

15. Which word uses -er in the same way as in the word tougher?
    (a) flower   (b) blender
    (c) cuter   (d) shower

16. Choose the correct spelling of the word.
    The ending of the story was _____ because unicorns do not really exist.
    (a) illogical   (b) ilogical
    (c) illogikal   (d) illojical

17. Choose the best word to fill in the blank.
    Jess sang _____ than Justin. (comparative)
    (a) most graceful
    (b) more gracefullest
    (c) most gracefullest
    (d) more gracefully

DIRECTIONS (Qs. 18 to 20): Read the passage carefully and answer the following questions.

Abraham Lincoln was elected as the 16th President of the United States in 1860. He did many things as President. Many people think he was the best American President of all time. He is most remembered for freeing the slaves. He was President of the United States during the time the Civil War was fought. The Civil War was fought between the Northern and Southern states.

18. How many Presidents were there before Abraham Lincoln?

    (a) 16 (b) 15
    (c) 14 (d) 13

19. What is Abraham Lincoln most remembered for?

    (a) Freeing slaves
    (b) Doing many things
    (c) Becoming President during the war
    (d) None of these

20. Who fought in the Civil War?

    (a) British
    (b) Spanish
    (c) Northern and Southern states
    (d) All of the above

21. Those boys answered all the questions smartly in class this morning.

    What word would you use as a substitute for the words 'those boys'?

    (a) he (b) she
    (c) me (d) they

22. Taught / school / he / in / us / English / the

    Which of the following is the best rearrangement of the words given above?

    (a) He the us taught in English school.
    (b) He taught us English in the school.
    (c) Taught us is he English the school.
    (d) Us taught the he English in school.

23. Which one from the following is not a noun?

    (a) Tail (b) Tell
    (c) Beak (d) Head

DIRECTIONS (Qs. 24 & 25): Read the sentences carefully and identify the noun marked in bold.

24. Cutlery is made of **steel**.

    (a) Proper noun
    (b) Collective noun
    (c) Common noun
    (d) Material noun

———————— Space for Rough Work ————————

25. I was very naughty in my **childhood**.

    (a) Abstract noun

    (b) Collective noun

    (c) Common noun

    (d) Material noun

DIRECTIONS (Qs. 26 & 27): Choose the correct word to complete the sentence.

26. We have a maid. The maid is honest.

    (a) We have a maid he is honest.

    (b) We have a maid who is honest.

    (c) We have a maid whom is honest.

    (d) We have a maid that is honest.

27. You are crazy, if you _____ I will have a pet snake.

    (a) trudge   (b) swam

    (c) wait   (d) think

28. Choose the correct adjective to complete the sentence.

    Neither Amar nor Anil likes to talk in front of a _____ group.

    (a) large   (b) nice

    (c) police   (d) dry

DIRECTIONS (Qs. 29 & 30): Choose the correct conjunctions to complete the sentence.

29. The bus stopped _____ the man got off.

    (a) and   (b) but

    (c) or   (d) so

30. We stayed at home _____ watched a film.

    (a) and   (b) but

    (c) or   (d) so

DIRECTIONS (Qs. 31 & 32): Choose the correct preposition to complete the sentence.

31. I'll be ready to leave _____ about twenty minutes.

    (a) in   (b) on

    (c) at   (d) with

32. He usually travels to Philadelphia _____ train.
    (a) in (b) on
    (c) by (d) with

33. Change the underlined proper noun to a common noun in the following sentence.
    We went to the <u>Golden Gate Park</u> last weekend.
    (a) city (b) park
    (c) team (d) country

34. Replace the noun in the bracket with a correct object pronoun.
    She is going to circus with (Henry).
    (a) he (b) you
    (c) him (d) himself

35. My family often ___ out for dinner.
    (a) go (b) goes
    (c) going (d) gone

36. He _____ watch T.V. on Saturdays.
    (a) doesn't (b) don't
    (c) does (d) doing

DIRECTIONS (Qs. 37 & 38): Choose the correct type of sentence.

37. Are Jessica and Lily sisters?
    (a) Declarative
    (b) Imperative
    (c) Exclamatory
    (d) Interrogative

38. I hope it snows ten inches on Saturday!
    (a) Exclamatory
    (b) Imperative
    (c) Interrogative
    (d) Declarative

DIRECTIONS (Qs. 39 & 40): Complete the sentence using the word or set of words for each blank that best fits the meaning of the sentence as a whole.

39. Unlike the actual building, which was quite sturdy, Cam's model of the building was _____.
    (a) plastic (b) stable
    (c) false (d) fragile

40. The gymnast was very _____, but her younger sister was completely _____.
    (a) heavy ... weighty
    (b) hollow ... skinny
    (c) flexible ... rigid
    (d) soft ... crafty

OLYMPIAD Mock Test 5

Name: _____
Number of Questions : 40
Max. Marks : 40
Time : 2 Hours

There is no negative marking in the test.

DIRECTIONS (Qs. 1 & 2): Choose the correct answer.

1. Which one from the following is not a noun?
   (a) Dancer   (b) Painter
   (c) Singer   (d) Hotter

2. Which one from the following is not a noun?
   (a) Belt   (b) Black
   (c) Shoe   (d) Lace

DIRECTIONS (Qs. 3 & 4): Join the following pairs of sentences by using a suitable relative pronoun.

3. This is the radio. I bought it last month.
   (a) This is the radio whom I bought it last month.
   (b) This is the radio who I bought it last month.
   (c) This is the radio that I bought last month.
   (d) This is the radio I bought it last month.

4. The students were absent. Students were fined.
   (a) The students were absent who were fined.
   (b) The students were absent whom were fined.
   (c) The students were absent which were fined.
   (d) The students who were absent were fined.

―――― *Space for Rough Work* ――――

DIRECTION (Q. 5): Choose the correct verb to complete the sentence.

5. The ducks _____ in the pond.
   (a) trudge   (b) swim
   (c) wait   (d) think

DIRECTIONS (Q. 6 to 8): Choose the correct word to complete the sentence.

6. The _____ officers created a road barrier to try to catch the criminal.
   (a) large   (b) nice
   (c) police   (d) strong

7. He is very rich _____ he doesn't spend a lot of money.
   (a) and   (b) but
   (c) or   (d) so

8. Do you want tea _____ coffee?
   (a) and   (b) but
   (c) or   (d) so

DIRECTIONS (Qs. 9 to 11): Choose the correct preposition to complete the sentence.

9. I think she spent the entire afternoon _____ the phone.
   (a) in   (b) on
   (c) at   (d) with

10. My fingers were injured so my sister had to write the note _____ me.
    (a) for   (b) on
    (c) at   (d) with

11. I am not interested _____ buying a new car now.
    (a) for   (b) on
    (c) in   (d) with

12. She hugged _____ her mom _____ dad.
    (a) whether, or
    (b) both, and
    (c) either, or
    (d) neither, nor

13. Change the underlined common noun to a proper noun in the following sentence.

    I bought some fruits for them.
    (a) dozens
    (b) pumpkin
    (c) apples and oranges
    (d) lemon

14. Change the underlined proper noun to a common noun in the following sentence.

    My friend wanted to join Foreign Language Club.
    (a) Country (b) People
    (c) Friend   (d) Club

15. Replace the noun in the bracket with a correct object pronoun. I saw (Kris and his dad) at the cricket match last night.
    (a) us   (b) them
    (c) you   (d) whom

16. Lisa never _____ her homework.
    (a) does   (b) doing
    (c) don't   (d) done

17. The shop _____ open until 12 o'clock.
    (a) do   (b) doesn't
    (c) does   (d) don't

18. A complete sentence must have a
    (a) subject and article
    (b) predicate and conjunction
    (c) conjunction and article
    (d) subject and predicate

DIRECTIONS (Qs. 19 & 20): Choose the word that is most nearly opposite in meaning to the word in capital letters.

19. CAPTIVITY
    (a) Slavery   (b) Permission
    (c) Freedom   (d) Limitation

20. REVEAL
    (a) Develop   (b) Showcase
    (c) Cover   (d) Thwart

21. Choose the correct synonym for the following word.

    HUGE
    (a) Light   (b) Tiny
    (c) Determined (d) Giant

22. Choose the correct description for the word given.

    DEFINITION

    (a) Baby sheep: lamb
    (b) Baby duck : cub
    (c) Baby cow : chicken
    (d) Baby lion : calf

23. Choose the correct word or phrase to complete the idiomatic phrase in the question.

    I think I understand the nuts and _____ of the operation.

    (a) screws (b) hammer
    (c) nails   (d) bolts

24. Choose the correct word or phrase to complete the idiomatic phrase in the question.

    Just a moment, I've got the answer on the ___ of my tongue.

    (a) top   (b) tap
    (c) tip   (d) back

25. The car in front of our scooter stopped abruptly. Since we were not prepared for that, we banged hard into it!

    The word abruptly as used in the sentence above, means_____

    (a) slowly, without hurry
    (b) suddenly, without warning
    (c) loudly, with a hard bang
    (d) quietly, in an unusual manner

26. Find the correct answer.

    (a) There going two help us.
    (b) They are going to help us.
    (c) Going to help her to us.
    (d) None of the above

27. Find the correct answer.

    (a) John washd the cars yesterdae.
    (b) John washed the car yesterday.
    (c) John washed yesterday the cars.
    (d) None of the above.

28. Arrange the sentence properly and choose the correct option.

    Are/harmless/to people/most bats

    (a) Most bats are harmless to people.
    (b) Bats are most people harmless.
    (c) Harmless to people are most bats.
    (d) None of the above

DIRECTIONS (Qs. 29 to 31): Complete the sentence using the word or set of words for each blank that best fits the meaning of the sentence as a whole.

29. Jackie is full of _____ and believes she can achieve almost any goal she sets for herself.

    (a) confidence (b) courage
    (c) concern   (d) comfort

30. While Johnny is not _____, he is not necessarily _____, either.

    (a) hungry ... tired
    (b) tall ... short
    (c) smart ... intelligent
    (d) fat ... thick

31. Although the message was meant to be _____, I don't mind if you tell it to your friends.

    (a) special   (b) secret
    (c) permanent   (d) educational

DIRECTIONS (Qs. 32 to 39): Read the passage. Then answer the questions below.

Lilly loves her new town. She loves the mall. She loves the parks. She also loves her school. Most of all, Lilly loves the seasons. In her old town, it was hot all of the time.

Sometimes it is cold in Lilly's new town. Once in a while it snows. Lilly has never seen snow before. So for her, the snow is exciting as well as very beautiful. Lilly has to wear gloves to keep her hands warm. She also wears a scarf around her neck.

———————— *Space for Rough Work* ————————

In spring, flowers bloom and the trees turn green with new leaves. Pollen falls on the cars and windowsills and makes Lilly sneeze. People work in their yards and mow their grass.

In summer, Lilly wears her old shorts and sandals- the same ones she used to wear in her old town. It's hot outside, and dogs lie in the shade. Lilly and her friends go to a pool or play in the water sprinkler. Her father cooks hamburgers on the grill for dinner.

Lilly's favourite season is autumn. In autumn, the leaves on the trees turn yellow, gold, red, and orange. Halloween comes in autumn, and this is Lilly's favourite holiday. Every Halloween, Lilly wears a costume. Last year she wore a mouse costume. This year she will wear a fish costume.

One evening in autumn, Lilly and her mom sat together on the porch. Mom told Lilly that autumn is also called "fall". This is a good idea, Lilly thinks, because in fall all of the leaves fall down from the trees.

32. Which of the following words best describes the way Lilly feels about living in her new town?

(a) Skeptical, meaning questioning or showing doubt

(b) Apprehensive, meaning anxious or worried

(c) Overjoyed, meaning extremely happy

(d) Content, meaning satisfied with what one is or has

33. This passage is mainly about
    (a) Lilly's favourite season.
    (b) Lilly and the four seasons.
    (c) Lilly's favourite activities during winter.
    (d) Lilly's favourite Halloween costumes.

34. What is Lilly's favourite thing about her new town?
    (a) Her school
    (b) Going to the pool
    (c) The food
    (d) The seasons

35. In paragraph 2 the author writes, "She also wears a scarf around her neck." What is the best way to rewrite this sentence while keeping its original meaning?
    (a) In addition, she wears a scarf around her neck.
    (b) However, she wears a scarf around her neck.
    (c) Nevertheless, she wears a scarf around her neck.
    (d) As a result, she wears a scarf around her neck.

36. Which of the following best describes the structure of this passage?
    (a) The author talks about Lily's new town, and then talks about how the seasons are changing.
    (b) The author introduces Lilly, and then describes her in relation to the four seasons.
    (c) The author introduces Lilly, and then explains why autumn is her favourite season.
    (d) The author discusses the four seasons, and then describes which one Lilly likes, the best.

37. How is Lilly's new town different from her old town?
    I.   It snows in her new town.
    II. Lilly wears different summer clothes in her new town.
    III. Lilly wears a Halloween costume in her new town.
    (a) I only
    (b) I and II only
    (c) II and III only
    (d) I, II, and III

─────── Space for Rough Work ───────

38. Based on information in paragraph 5, which of the following costumes is Lilly most likely to wear next year?

    (a) A princess costume
    (b) A fairy costume
    (c) A ghost costume
    (d) A bird costume

39. Based on information in the passage, we can understand that, which season has two names?

    (a) Spring   (b) Summer
    (c) Fall   (d) Winter

40. Use comas to separate items in a list of three or more.

    Carlos wants to visit Paris Italy Germany and China.

    (a) Carlos wants to visit Paris -Italy -Germany and China.
    (b) Carlos wants to visit Paris, Italy, Germany, and China.
    (c) Carlos wants to visit Paris; Italy; Germany and China.
    (d) Carlos wants to visit Paris. Italy. Germany and China.

──────────── Space for Rough Work ────────────

MATHEMATICS MOCK TEST 1-5

OLYMPIAD Mock Test 1

Name : _____
Number of Questions : 35
There is no negative marking in the test.

Max. Marks : 35
Time : 2 Hours

1. Which one of the following numbers should be added to 563876 such that the sum becomes twice of 986456?
   (a) 1409063   (b) 1409036
   (c) 1049036   (d) 1400936

2. Find the greatest number that divides 57 and 67 leaving 7 as remainder.
   (a) 3000   (b) 10
   (c) 665   (d) 50

3. Which one of the following Roman Numerals is correct for 985 ?
   (a) MCLXXXV   (b) CMLXXVX
   (c) CMLXXXV   (d) MLCXXXV

4. Which number is a common factor of 42 and 70 ?
   (a) 14   (b) 10
   (c) 21   (d) 8

5. Match the following columns.

Column - I	Column - II
(A) Cube	(1) ⬚
(B) Cone	(2) ⬚
(C) Cylinder	(3) ⬚
(D) Cuboid	(4) ⬚

───── Space for Rough Work ─────

	A	B	C	D
(a)	3	1	4	2
(b)	4	3	2	1
(c)	3	4	1	2
(d)	4	2	3	1

6. Look at the numbers shown below. Subtract 2 from the 3rd number from the left. The answer is the same as the _____ number from the right.

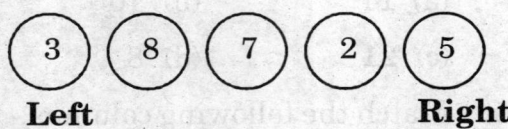

Left   **Right**

(a) 1st   (b) 2nd

(c) 3rd   (d) 4th

7. Anjali put 50 pickles on 10 sandwiches. She put the same number of pickles on each sandwich. Which of the following number sentence can be used to find how many pickles Anjali put on each sandwich?

(a) 50 − 10 = 40

(b) 50 × 10 = 500

(c) 50 + 10 = 60

(d) 50 ÷ 10 = 5

8. Consider the following statements.

Statement 1 : 6.7, 67, 0.67 and 0.067 are unlike decimals.

Statement 2 : $\frac{5}{2}, \frac{5}{2}, \frac{5}{9}$ and $\frac{5}{3}$ are like fractions.

Now, choose the correct option.

(a) Statement 1 is true and 2 is false.

(b) Statement 1 is false and 2 is true.

(c) Both statements 1 and 2 are true.

(d) Both statements 1 and 2 are false.

Space for Rough Work

9. What fraction of the figure is unshaded ?

(a) Three eighths
(b) One quarter
(c) One half
(d) One third

10. Raghu is 21 years old and Kavita is 22 years old. Write the sum of their ages in Roman systems.

(a) XXXIII (b) XLIII
(c) LIII   (d) XLCIII

11. The product of place values of two '9's in 89091 is _____.

(a) 81   (b) 81,000
(c) 8,10,000 (d) None of these

12. Which digit should come in place of ☐, so that the following addition is correct ?

```
   8 7 6 5
 + 7 ☐ 6
 ─────────
   9 5 5 1
```

(a) 6 (b) 9
(c) 8 (d) 5

13. Guru put a number into the 'START' box of the sentence below.

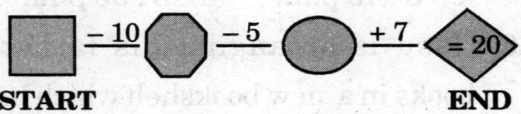

The "END" number was 20. What number did Guru put into the 'START' box ?

(a) 20 (b) 28
(c) 35 (d) 42

———————— Space for Rough Work ————————

14. Each part on the number line drawn below is of 1 cm. The sum of AC + DE + GJ is equal to

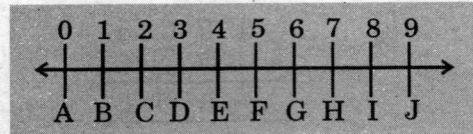

(a) AF (b) BH
(c) DG (d) FJ

15. The time 1 hour 28 minutes after 4 : 15 p.m. is

(a) 3 : 58 p.m. (b) 5 : 30 p.m.
(c) 5 : 43 p.m. (d) 3 : 30 p.m.

16. Vasu is arranging his father's books in a new bookshelf which has 5 shelves. After putting 12 books in each shelf, he finds that 9 books are still left outside. How many books are there in total ?

(a) 69 (b) 75
(c) 21 (d) 108

17. State which of the following are true/false.

A : Area of square = side × side
B : Perimeter of rectangle = length + breadth
C : A triangle having two of its sides equal is an isosceles triangles.
D : A triangle having all its sides different is an equilateral triangle.

(a) TTFF (b) TFTF
(c) TFFT (d) FFTT

18. ABC is a triangle. If ∠ABC = 64° and ∠BCA = 78°, then ∠BCA is a

(a) Acute angle (b) Obtuse angle
(c) Right angle (d) All of these

19. There are two rods of equal length. One rod is bent into a square shape. Length of the one side of the square is 9 cm. Other rod is bent into a rectangle shape whose length is 11 cm and breadth is 7. Which encloses more area?

(a) Rectangle

(b) Square

(c) Both are equal

(d) All of these

20. I have 6 faces, all of which are squares of same size. I am ____. I have ____ vertices ____ edges.

   (a) cuboid, 12, 8
   (b) cube, 8, 12
   (c) sphere, 0, 1
   (d) none of these

21. Kamal plans to cover the boundary of park with tiles. What should Kamal know to make sure he buys enough tiles ?

   (a) Length of park
   (b) The perimeter of the park
   (c) Area of park
   (d) None of these

22. Find the perimeter of the shaded part of the given figure.

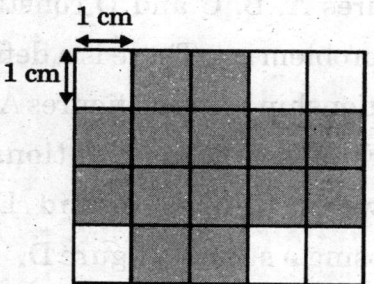

   (a) 12 cm   (b) 14 cm
   (c) 16 cm   (d) 18 cm

23. A _____ is a chord that passes through the centre of the circle.

   (a) radius   (b) chord
   (c) centre   (d) diameter

24. Find the missing length of the following figure.

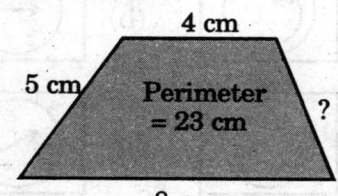

   (a) 6 cm   (b) 4 cm
   (c) 2 cm   (d) 5 cm

───────── Space for Rough Work ─────────

25. Direction: Given below question consists of two sets of figures. Figures A, B, C and D constitute the problem set. There is a definite relationship between figures A and B. Find a similar relationship between figures C and D by choosing a suitable figure D.

Problem set :

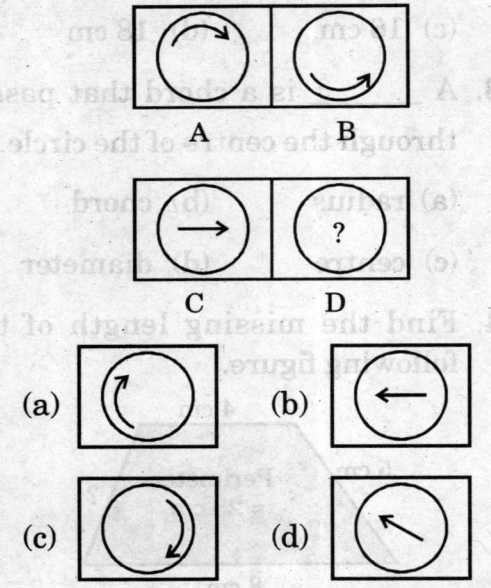

26. If radius of the circle is first odd prime number, then find its diameter.

(a) 15 units (b) 10 units
(c) 6 units (d) 9 units

27. If 500 g of apples cost ₹ 50, what is the cost of 1 kg apples?

(a) ₹ 75 (b) ₹ 100
(c) ₹ 50 (d) ₹ 95

28. Vessels P and Q contain water as shown below. The amount of water in them is marked in millilitres.

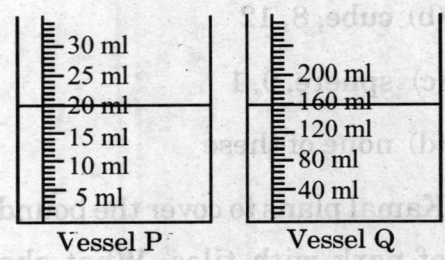

If the water in vessels P and Q is completely poured into a third vessel R, how many litres of water will there be in vessel R?

(a) 0.12 litre (b) 0.18 litre
(c) 0.2 litre (d) 20 litres

29. A bus runs 234 km in 18 litres of petrol. Find the distance it will run in 45 litres of petrols.
   (a) 550 km   (b) 575 km
   (c) 585 km   (d) 595 km

DIRECTIONS (Qs. 30 to 33) : In the following bar graph students from different classes who participated in a competition has been shown. See the graph and answer the questions that follow.

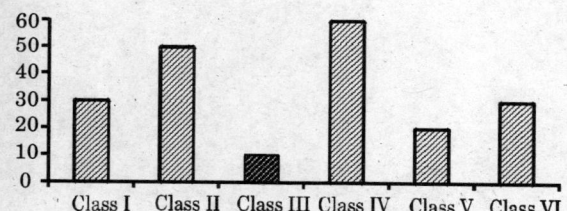

30. How many students participated in the competition ?
   (a) 150   (b) 170
   (c) 200   (d) 250

31. What scale has been chosen in making the bar graph ?
   (a) 1 cm = 1 student
   (b) 1 cm = 10 students
   (c) 1 cm = 20 students
   (d) 1 cm = 30 students

32. How many students participated in the competition from class IV?
   (a) 30   (b) 40
   (c) 50   (d) 60

33. Name the classes from which same number of students participated in the competition ?
   (a) Class I and Class II
   (b) Class I and Class VI
   (c) Class II and Class III
   (d) Class VI and Class V

34. Complete the pattern given below in the following questions.

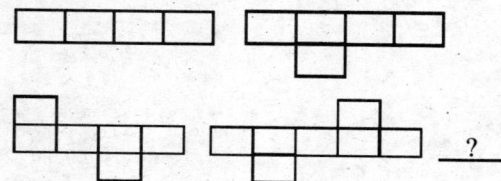

———— Space for Rough Work ————

(a)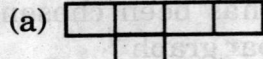

(b)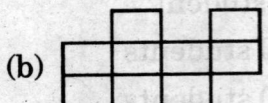

(c)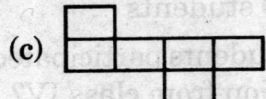

(d)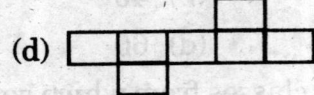

35. Identify the rule for the given pattern in the following question.

   3, 6, 12, 24, 48, 96

   (a) Multiply by 3
   (b) Multiply by 2
   (c) Multiply by 4
   (d) Add 3

OLYMPIAD Mock Test 2

Name: _____
Number of Questions : 35
There is no negative marking in the test.

Max. Marks : 35
Time : 2 Hours

1. Sanjay painted $\frac{1}{3}$ of a wall blue, $\frac{2}{7}$ green and the rest of it yellow. The part of the wall painted yellow is
   (a) $\frac{13}{21}$ (b) $\frac{1}{4}$
   (c) $\frac{3}{10}$ (d) $\frac{8}{21}$

2. The decimal form of the number given by $\frac{9}{100000}+\frac{7}{1000}+\frac{5}{100}+\frac{4}{10}$ is
   (a) 0.45709 (b) 0.40579
   (c) 0.90754 (d) 0.97054

3. The product of two numbers is 476. If one number is 34, what is the other number?

   (a) 442 (b) 104
   (c) 24   (d) 14

4. Nirmal rode his bike on two days. He rode a total of 12 kilometres in two days. On the first day, Nirmal rode $7\frac{1}{2}$ kilometres. How many kilometres did Nirmal ride on the second day?
   (a) $19\frac{1}{2}$ kilometres
   (b) $5\frac{1}{2}$ kilometres
   (c) $4\frac{1}{2}$ kilometres
   (d) $3\frac{1}{2}$ kilometres

─────── *Space for Rough Work* ───────

5. Christina has ₹ 235 more than the money Jack has. If Jack has ₹ 200, how much money do they have together?

   (a) ₹ 625 (b) ₹ 635
   (c) ₹ 630 (d) ₹ 650

6. On Sports Day, 161 children are in the school playground. They are standing in 7 equal rows. How many children are there in each row?

   (a) 22 (b) 23
   (c) 25 (d) 52

7. Which figure represents $\frac{1}{4}$th of the shaded part?

   (a)  (b)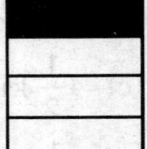

   (c) (d)

8. How many more boxes must be shaded in order to have $\frac{1}{4}$ of the figure shaded?

   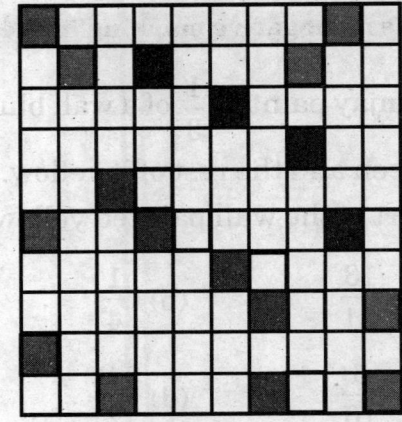

   (a) 7 (b) 8
   (c) 18 (d) 25

9. The value of (1 + .1 + .01 + .001) is

   (a) 1.003 (b) 1.111
   (c) 1.011 (d) 1.001

───────── Space for Rough Work ─────────

Mock Test-2

M-11

10. Amisha makes a figure and divides it into some equal parts. Now she shades few parts, thus, decimal representation for the shaded part is 0.03. How many parts of the figure is unshaded?

(a) 3 (b) 30
(c) 97 (d) 7

11. Which square must be shaded so that the figure has a line of symmetry?

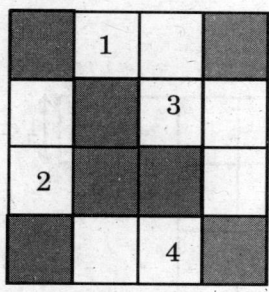

(a) 1 (b) 2
(c) 3 (d) 4

12. Match the following.

Column-I Column-II

(A) 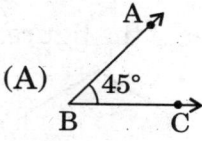 (1) Right angle

(B) 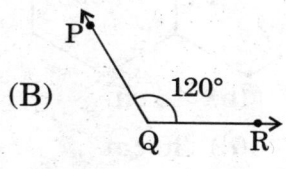 (2) Acute angle

(C) 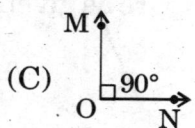 (3) Straight angle

(D) 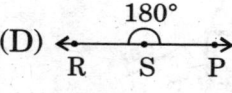 (4) Obtuse angle

    A B C D
(a) 2 1 4 3
(b) 1 2 3 4
(c) 2 4 1 3
(d) 1 3 2 4

———————— Space for Rough Work ————————

13. In the following figure, there are three equal hexagons whose each side is equal. If length of one side is 3 cm, find the perimeter of the figure.

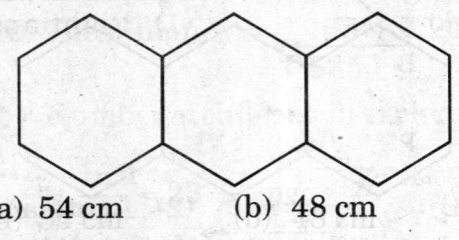

(a) 54 cm (b) 48 cm
(c) 42 cm (d) 36 cm

14. The perimetre of the figure as given below is

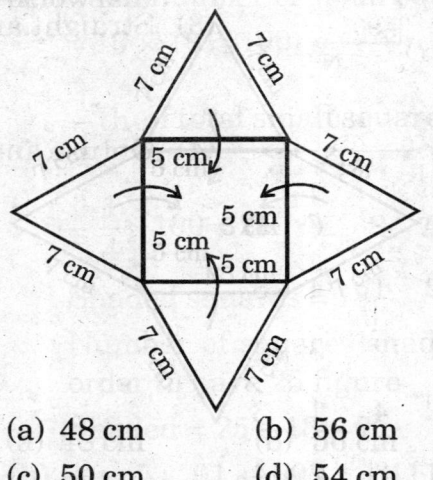

(a) 48 cm (b) 56 cm
(c) 50 cm (d) 54 cm

15. Which of the following figures has a perimeter that is $\frac{1}{4}$th of 56 cm?

(a)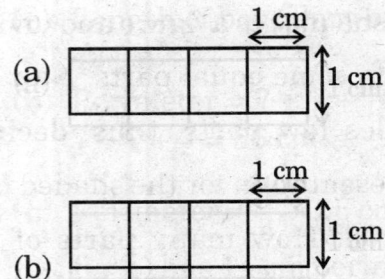

(b)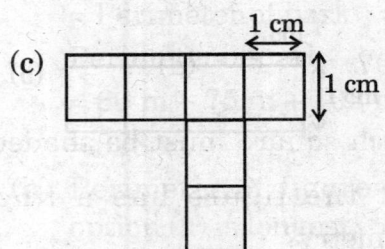

(c)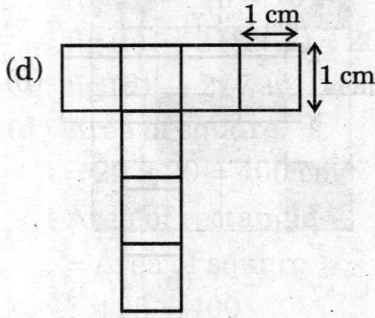

(d)

16. Tina found a triangular flag. She traced the flag on graph paper, as shown.

Space for Rough Work

Mock Test-2

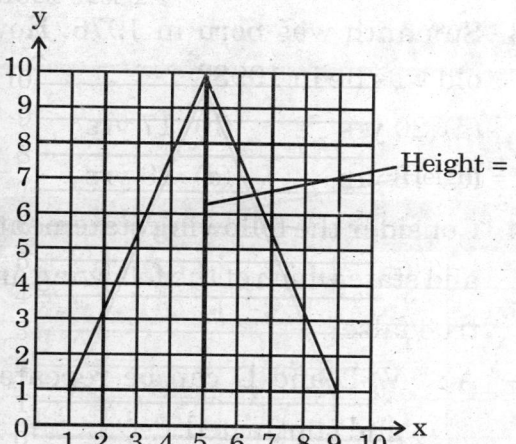

What was the height of the triangular flag?

(a) 4 units (b) 8 units
(c) 9 units (d) 10 units

17. Raghu walks around a park every day. How far does he walk in one round?

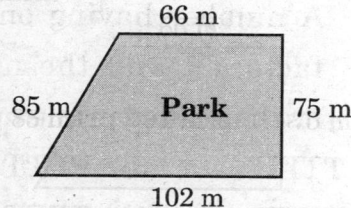

(a) 198 m (b) 298 m
(c) 228 m (d) 328 m

18. Which of the following shapes has the greatest perimeter?

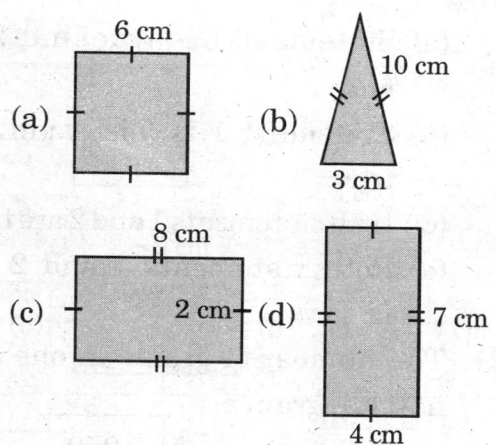

19. In the diagram, the square and the rectangle have the same area.

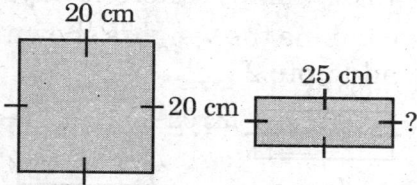

Find the breadth of the rectangle.

(a) 8 cm (b) 10 cm
(c) 15 cm (d) 16 cm

20. Consider the following statements.

Statement 1: The diameter is the longest chord in a circle.

Statement 2: A polygon made of 4 straight lines is called triangle.

Now, choose the correct option.

(a) Statement 1 is true and 2 is false.
(b) Statement 1 is false and 2 is true.
(c) Both statements 1 and 2 are true.
(d) Both statements 1 and 2 are false.

21. The number of grams in one and half kilogram are _____.
(a) 1000   (b) 1050
(c) 1500   (d) 1005

22. In how many different ways can we combine the weights shown here to add upto 2 kg?

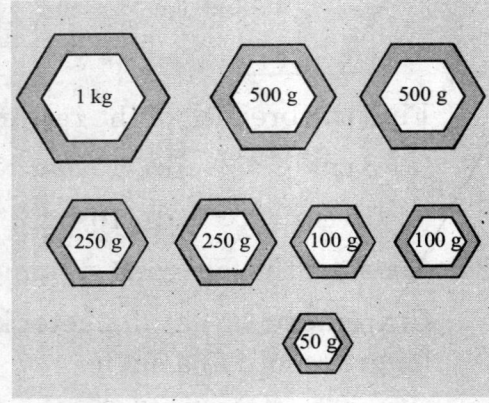

(a) 2 ways   (b) 3 ways
(c) 4 ways   (d) 5 ways

23. Sumanth was born in 1976. How old was he in 1993?
(a) 20 yrs   (b) 17 yrs
(c) 18 yrs   (d) 19 yrs

24. Consider the following statements and state which of the following are true/false.
A : V, L and D can be repeated and subtracted.
B : Adding 1 to a number gives its predecessor.
C : A fraction is in its simplest form, if numerator and denominator do not have any common factor other than 1.
D : A number having only two factors 1 and the number itself is called prime number.
(a) TTFF   (b) FFTT
(c) TFTF   (d) TFFT

25. Find the dividend, when divisor = 23, quotient = 35 and remainder = 21.

(a) 518 (b) 826
(c) 805 (d) 483

26. How much does the  cost?

(a) ₹ 100 (b) ₹ 320
(c) ₹ 200 (d) ₹ 240

27. The given bar graph shows the height of five children. What is the difference between the height of the tallest child and the shortest child?

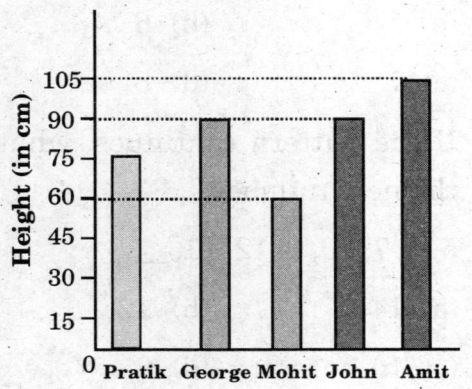

(a) 45 cm (b) 30 cm
(c) 60 cm (d) 105 cm

DIRECTIONS (28 to 30): Study the graph and answer the questions that follow.

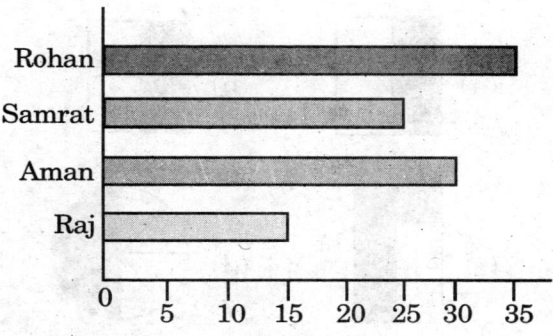

28. _____ has 5 toy cars more than Samrat.

(a) Raj (b) Rohan
(c) Aman (d) None of these

29. _____ has 2 times more toy cars than Raj.

(a) Aman (b) Rohan
(c) Samrat (d) None of these

———————— Space for Rough Work ————————

30. The four boys have _____ toy cars altogether.
    (a) 95   (b) 100
    (c) 105 (d) 110

31. Find the odd one out.

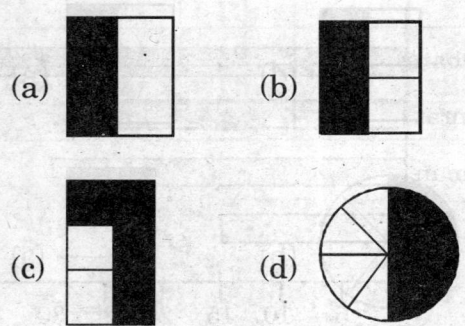

32. In its first year of business, a company had 5 employees. In its second year, there were 25 employees, and in its third year, there were 125 employees. If the pattern continues, how many employees will the company has in fourth year?
    (a) 250   (b) 625
    (c) 3,125 (d) 15,625

33. Riya is 17th from the front in a queue. She is 19th from the end. Then how many students are there in a queue?
    (a) 35   (b) 36
    (c) 7   (d) 20

34. Find the missing number in Fig. (X).

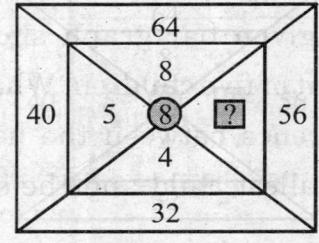

Figure X

    (a) 5   (b) 6
    (c) 7   (d) 8

35. If the pattern continues, what is the next number ?
    5, 8, 7, 10, 9, 12, 11, ____
    (a) 14   (b) 12
    (c) 10   (d) 8

OLYMPIAD Mock Test 3

Name : _____
Number of Questions : 35
Max. Marks : 35
Time : 2 Hours

There is no negative marking in the test.

1. $3 \times 0.0001 + 4 \times 0.001 + 7 \times 0.01 + 9 \times 0.1 + 7 \times 1$ = _____ ?
   (a) 34.797
   (b) 7.9743
   (c) 0.34797
   (d) 3.4797

2. Which one of the following numbers should be inserted in the blank box in the following pyramid ?

   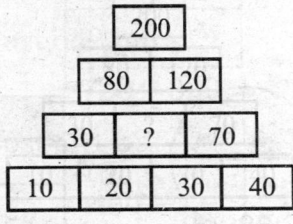

   (a) 154
   (b) 85
   (c) 26
   (d) 50

3. Which one of the following symbols should be inserted between L and I in the Roman numeral XLIII such that it can represent 48?
   (a) X
   (b) V
   (c) L
   (d) C

4. Find the value of
   $7432 - 2684 \div 4 \times 3 + 3261$
   (a) 7432
   (b) 7655
   (c) 8680
   (d) 10916

5. $6 + 6 + 6 + \ldots$ 695 times = ?
   (a) 4170
   (b) 4200
   (c) 4270
   (d) 4110

6. Which digit should come in place of □, so that following multiplication is correct ?

   ```
       4 □ 8
   ×       8
   ---------
     3 9 8 4
   ```

   (a) 1
   (b) 5
   (c) 7
   (d) 9

———— Space for Rough Work ————

7. When Rahul multiplies A by 59, the product he gets 322376. Find the value of A.
   (a) 5406 (b) 4123
   (c) 3214 (d) 5464

8. Match the following columns :

Column - I	Column - II
(A) $6\dfrac{2}{3} - \dfrac{7}{9} - 2\dfrac{1}{6}$	(1) $2\dfrac{7}{8}$
(B) $\dfrac{5}{8} - \dfrac{1}{4} + \dfrac{5}{2}$	(2) $3\dfrac{3}{4}$
(C) $3\dfrac{2}{3} + 4\dfrac{2}{3} - 2\dfrac{5}{6}$	(3) $3\dfrac{13}{18}$
(D) $2\dfrac{3}{4} + 4\dfrac{1}{2} - 3\dfrac{1}{2}$	(4) $5\dfrac{1}{2}$

   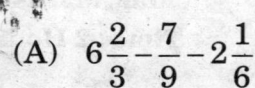

	A	B	C	D
(a)	1	3	2	4
(b)	3	1	4	2
(c)	1	2	3	4
(d)	3	4	1	2

9. Which one of the following is true for 0.003?
   (a) Three - tenth
   (b) Three - hundredth
   (c) Three - thousandth
   (d) Three-ten thousandth

10. Which one of the following is the equivalent decimal of 623.523?
    (a) 623.52300 (b) 623.5023
    (c) 62.3523   (d) 0.623523

11. Sum of 2 hrs 45 min. 23 sec and 3 hrs 35 min. 53 sec. is
    (a) 6 hrs 20 min. 16 sec.
    (b) 6 hrs 21 min. 16 sec.
    (c) 5 hrs 82 min. 75 sec.
    (d) 5 hrs 21 min. 16 sec.

12. The fraction represented by shaded region in the following figure is equivalent to

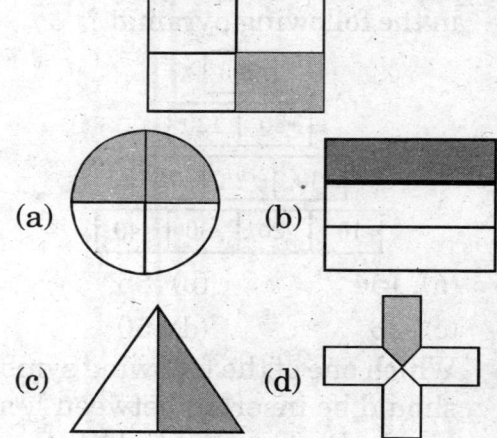

Space for Rough Work

13. Which of the following is not true ?
    (a) 0.4 + 0.4 + 0.4 = 1.2
    (b) 2.1 − 1.11 = 0.99
    (c) 0.7 + 0.7 + 0.7 + 0.7 = 4 × 0.7
    (d) 0.36 − 0.6 = 0.30

14. The diagram shows a straight line KLMN.

    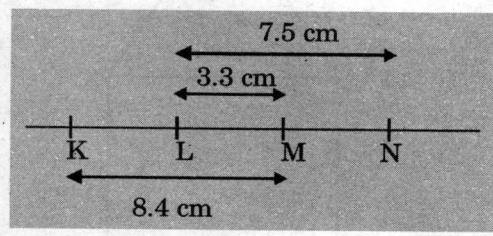

    What is the distance between points K and N?
    (a) 11.7 cm   (b) 12.6 cm
    (c) 15.9 cm   (d) 19.2 cm

15. Write the least 2-digit number that has 2, 5 and 8 as factors.
    (a) 80   (b) 40
    (c) 16   (d) 10

16. Ravi wrote two digits of a 3 - digit number on the blackboard as shown below.

    | 1 | ? | 3 |

    Find the missing digit if it has 11 and 13 as factors.
    (a) 2   (b) 4
    (c) 6   (d) 8

17. Which of the following statements is true/false?
    A : A line segment joining any two points on the circle is chord of the circle.
    B : A ray has a fixed length.
    C : The diameter passes through the centre of the circle.
    D : Two radii of a circle are of different length
    Now, choose the correct option.
    (a) TTFF   (b) TFTF
    (c) TFFT   (d) FFTT

18. The perimeters of square A and rectangle B are equal. Find the sides of square A.

    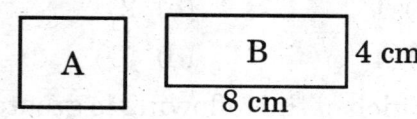

    (a) 6 cm   (b) 8 cm
    (c) 32 cm   (d) 36 cm

Space for Rough Work

19. Name the angle which measures between 0° and 90°.
    (a) Acute angle
    (b) Obtuse angle
    (c) Right angle
    (d) Straight angle

20. Which kind of triangle is given below?

    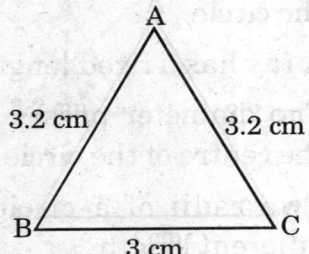

    (a) Equilateral triangle
    (b) Isosceles triangle
    (c) Scalene triangle
    (d) Irregular triangle

21. Which of the following is an even prime number?
    (a) 1   (b) 2
    (c) 4   (d) 5

22. Which of the following is greatest?
    (a) 0.106   (b) 0.9
    (c) 0.23   (d) 0.09

23. In the following figure BCDE is a square and ABE is an equilateral triangle. Find the perimeter of the figure given below.

    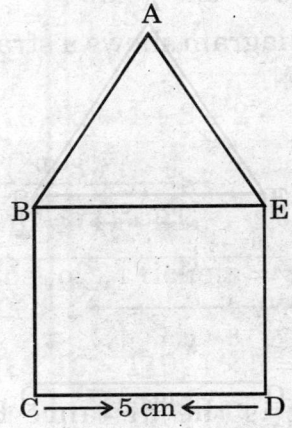

    (a) 20 cm   (b) 22 cm
    (c) 24 cm   (d) 25 cm

24. Mr. Gupta travelled 75 km 800 m by car and 1800 km 40 m by air. What distance did he travel in all?
    (a) 1875 km 840 m
    (b) 1675 km
    (c) 175800 km
    (d) 255840 km

Space for Rough Work

25. The following is the bill of clothes Mr. Verma bought from a shop.

Shirt	₹ 720
Pant	₹ 950
Tie	₹ 250

If he paid ₹ 2000, how much will he get back?

(a) ₹ 280 (b) ₹ 180
(c) ₹ 80   (d) ₹ 270

DIRECTIONS (26-28): Read the menu of a famous hotel and answer the following questions.

Menu			
Item	Cost (₹)	Item	Cost (₹)
Soup	300	Chips	100
Juice	100	Coffee	150
Pizza	370	Tea	80
Cutlet	500	Water bottle	50

26. If Sonia bought 2 soups, how much she has to pay?

(a) ₹ 300 (b) ₹ 420
(c) ₹ 600 (d) ₹ 700

27. Rohan has given a party to two of his friends. He bought 2 packets of chips, 1 pizza and 2 juices. How much he has to pay?

(a) ₹ 750 (b) ₹ 700
(c) ₹ 770 (d) ₹ 720

28. For buying 5 cups of tea and 1 pizza, Rohit should carry ___.

(a) ₹ 770 (b) ₹ 550
(c) ₹ 700 (d) ₹ 560

29. Consider the following statements.

Statement 1 : The product of the numbers does not change even if order of numbers is changed.

Statement 2 : 1 is the smallest prime number.

Now, choose the correct option.

(a) Statement 1 is false and 2 is true.
(b) Statement 1 is true and 2 is false.
(c) Both statements 1 and 2 are true.
(d) Both statements 1 and 2 are false.

30. How many minutes should be added to the time shown by the clock to make it quarter past four?

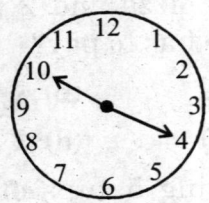

(a) 10 minutes (b) 15 minutes
(c) 25 minutes (d) 30 minutes

31. Complete the pattern in the given figure by selecting one of the figures from the four alternatives.

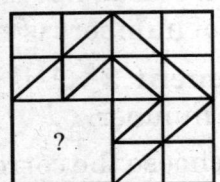

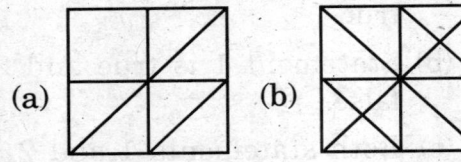

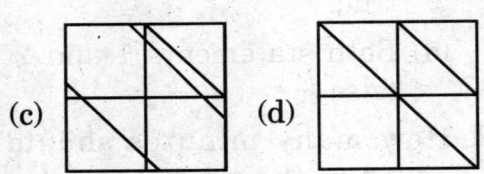

32. The figure X given below is incomplete. Which figure given in options is required to complete the figure?

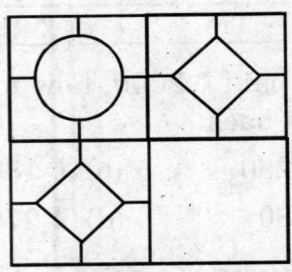

Fig. X

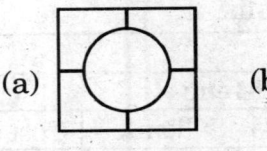 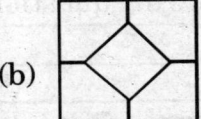

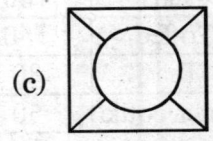 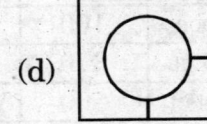

33. Saurav is building a pyramid. He uses 9 blocks in the first row, 7 blocks in the second row, and 5 blocks in the third row. If the pattern continues, how many blocks will he use in the fifth row?

Space for Rough Work

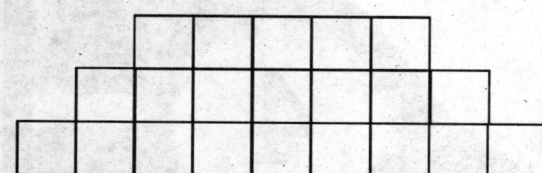

(a) 7   (b) 5
(c) 3   (d) 1

34. If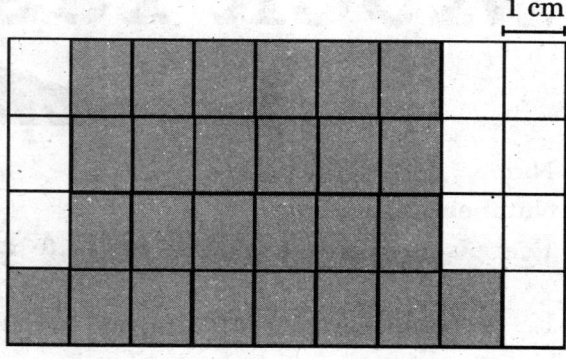

(a) 15   (b) 110
(c) 45   (d) 65

35. Find the area of shaded part in the figure below.

(a) 21 cm^2 (b) 25 cm^2
(c) 26 cm^2 (d) 29 cm^2

OLYMPIAD Mock Test 4

Name : _____
Number of Questions : 40
Max. Marks : 40
Time : 2 Hours

There is no negative marking in the test.

1. Arrange the following numerals in descending order.

    LXIV, LXVI, CLI, CXXXVII

    (a) LXIV, CLI, LXVICXXXVII
    (b) LXIV, LXVI, CLI, CXXXVII
    (c) CLI, LXVI, CXXXVII, LXIV
    (d) CLI, CXXXVII, LXVI, LXIV

2. The successor of a number is one more than the number and the predecessor is one less than the number. Which one of the following digits does not occur in the difference between the successor of 67854398 and the predecessor of 54677456 ?

    (a) 5   (b) 9
    (c) 1   (d) 7

3. A + B + 45896 = C + D. If C + D = 96023 + B, find the value of A.

    (a) 50120   (b) 50127
    (c) 30127   (d) 20127

4. In a magic box, if you put a number then the number is first added by 16 and reduced by 10 and then again it is reduced by 2 and added by 15. If Sameer puts 24 into the box what will be the result?

    (a) 43   (b) 33
    (c) 45   (d) 46

Space for Rough Work

5. If A is divided by B, then quotient is C and remainder is D, then find which one of the following is correct?

   (a) A = B × C × D
   (b) A < B × C + D
   (c) D < B
   (d) A = B × C + D

6. How many parts of the following figure would you like to shade such that the shaded part of the figure can represent unit fraction?

   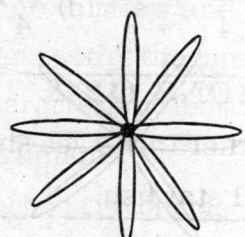

   (a) One part   (b) Two parts
   (c) Three parts (d) Four parts

7. John makes a rectangular figure and divides it into 100 equal parts. He shaded 3 parts out of every 10 parts. Find the correct expression for the shaded part.

   (a) $\dfrac{1}{100}$ (b) $\dfrac{10}{100}$
   (c) $\dfrac{3}{100}$ (d) $\dfrac{30}{100}$

8. How many parts should be shaded in the figure (ii) such that fractional representation of the shaded part becomes equivalent to the shaded part of figure (i)?

   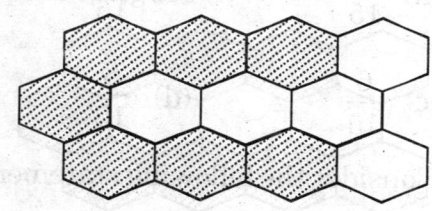
   Figure (i)

   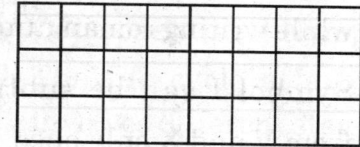
   Figure (ii)

   (a) 7 parts   (b) 14 parts
   (c) 21 parts   (d) All the parts

—————————— Space for Rough Work ——————————

9. What should be placed in the empty space so that the sum of the fraction on each side of the triangle is same?

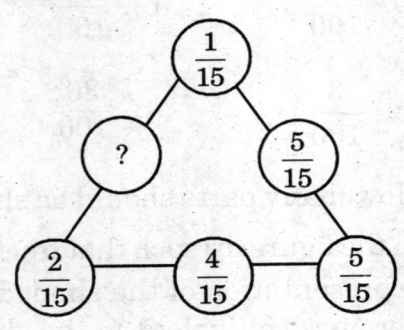

(a) $\dfrac{7}{15}$ (b) $\dfrac{9}{15}$

(c) $\dfrac{6}{15}$ (d) $\dfrac{8}{15}$

10. Consider the following statements?

(A) V, L, D are never subtracted while writing roman numerals.

(B) Symbol I can be subtracted from V and X only once.

(C) X cannot be subtracted from L.

(D) X can be repeated maximum 2 times.

Now, choose the correct option.

(a) TFTF   (b) TFFT
(c) TTFF   (d) FFTT

11. What is the fraction used to represent the shaded parts?

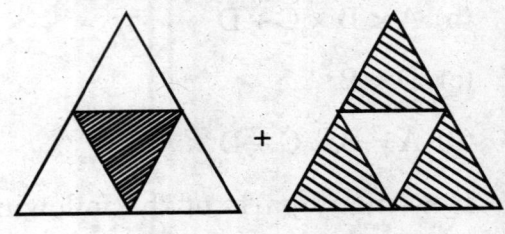

(a) $\dfrac{2}{4}+\dfrac{3}{4}$ (b) $\dfrac{1}{4}+\dfrac{3}{4}$

(c) $\dfrac{3}{4}+\dfrac{3}{4}$ (d) $\dfrac{1}{4}+\dfrac{1}{4}$

DIRECTIONS (12 & 13): In an aquarium there are 4 sea shells, 5 gold fishes and 1 star fish.

12. Which fraction represents the gold fish?

(a) $\dfrac{5}{10}$ (b) $\dfrac{1}{10}$

(c) $\dfrac{4}{10}$ (d) $\dfrac{3}{10}$

———— Space for Rough Work ————

13. Which of the following statements about gold fish is true ?

    (a) Half of the fish in aquarium are gold fish.

    (b) More than half of the fish in aquarium are gold fish.

    (c) None of the fish is gold fish.

    (d) All fishes are gold fish.

14. The given table shows the number of buttons that were made at a button factory each week for three weeks. Which of the following shows correct order of the week with the greatest number of buttons made to the week with the least number of buttons made?

Buttons Made	
Week	Number of Buttons
Week 1	84,503
Week 2	80,968
Week 3	84,551

    (a) Week 1, Week 3, Week 2

    (b) Week 2, Week 3, Week 1

    (c) Week 2, Week 1, Week 3

    (d) Week 3, Week 1, Week 2

15. Which digit should come in place of ☐, so that the following subtraction is correct ?

    ```
       5 6 3 8
     - 2 1 ☐ 9
     ─────────
       3 4 4 9
    ```

    (a) 7 (b) 8

    (c) 6 (d) 5

16. Match the following columns.

Column -I	Column-II
(A) Area of a square (4 cm)	(1) 14 cm
(B) Perimeter of rectangle (5 cm × 2 cm)	(2) 24 cm²

───── Space for Rough Work ─────

(C) Area of rectangle   (3) 10 cm

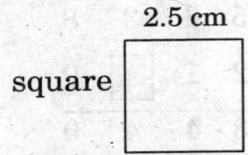

(D) Perimeter of   (4) 16 cm²

square  (with 2.5 cm label)

	A	B	C	D
(a)	4	2	1	3
(b)	2	4	3	1
(c)	4	1	2	3
(d)	2	3	4	1

17. Which number should come in place of □ ?

$$\frac{1}{7} + \frac{2}{7} + \frac{\square}{7} = 1\frac{3}{7}$$

(a) 1   (b) 2

(c) 3   (d) 7

18. The cake given in the picture is cut into 12 equal-sized pieces.

Geeta and her friends ate 9 pieces of the cake. Which fraction represents the amount of the original cake that was left?

(a) $\frac{3}{12}$ (b) $\frac{3}{9}$

(c) $\frac{6}{9}$ (d) $\frac{9}{12}$

19. Which of the following figures correctly shows a line of symmetry ?

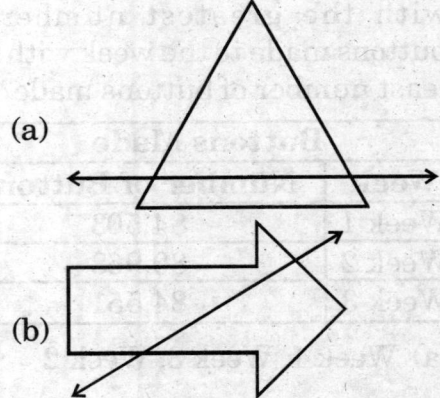

(a)

(b)

———————— Space for Rough Work ————————

(c)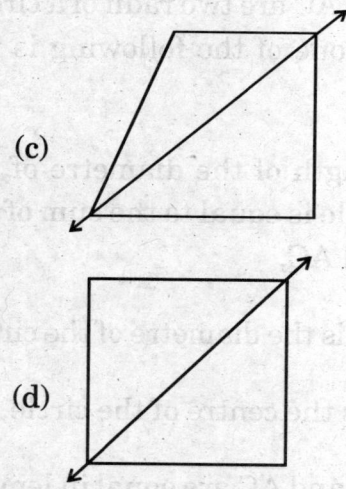

(d)

20. Which type of angle best describes angle Q?

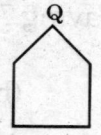

(a) Obtuse (b) Acute
(c) Right   (d) Straight

21. How many multiples of 10 are there from 20 to 150?

(a) 13   (b) 14
(c) 15   (d) 12

22. The following figure is an isosceles triangle. Why?

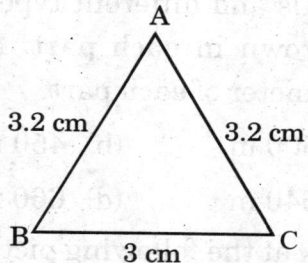

(a) Because it has two equal sides
(b) Because it has two different angles
(c) Because AB is greater than BC
(d) All of these

23. Consider the following statements.

Statement 1 : Triangles have only three angles, whereas quadrilateral has four angles.

Statement 2 : Sum of angles of a triangle is 360°.

(a) Statement 1 is false and 2 is true.
(b) Statement 1 is true and 2 is false.
(c) Both statements 1 and 2 are false.
(d) Both statements 1 and 2 are true.

———— Space for Rough Work ————

24. A farm land which is 350 m long and 150 m wide is divided into four equals and different types of crop is grown in each part. Find the perimeter of each part.

    (a) 500 m   (b) 450 m
    (c) 540 m   (d) 660 m

25. Look at the following picture.

    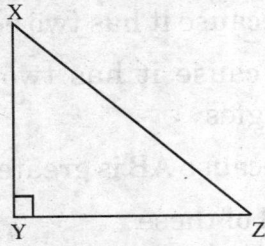

    Which one of the following is correct?

    (a) Both ∠X and ∠Z are acute angles.
    (b) ∠X is an acute angle whereas ∠Z is an obtuse angle.
    (c) ∠X is an obtuse angle whereas ∠Z is an acute angle.
    (d) Both ∠X and ∠Z are obtuse angles.

26. AB and AC are two radii of a circle. Which one of the following is not true?

    (a) Length of the diametre of the circle is equal to the sum of AB and AC.
    (b) BC is the diametre of the circle.
    (c) A is the centre of the circle.
    (d) AB and AC are equal in length.

27. The greatest number that divides 42 and 67 leaving 7 as remainder is

    (a) 7   (b) 5
    (c) 10   (d) 6

28. Simplify : $42 \div 7 \times 5 + 4 - 9$

    (a) 30   (b) 34
    (c) 25   (d) 45

29. If the length of rope needed to make border X is 14 cm, find the length of rope needed for border Y.

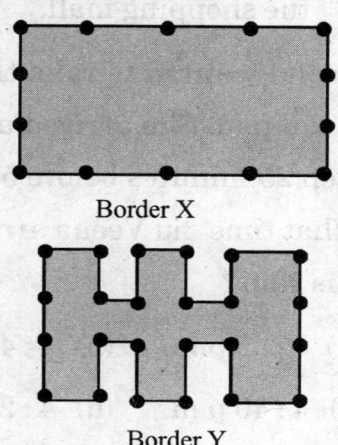

Border X

Border Y

(a) 16 cm (b) 20 cm
(c) 22 cm (d) 24 cm

30. Vessels P and Q contain water shown below. The amount of water in them is marked in millilitres.

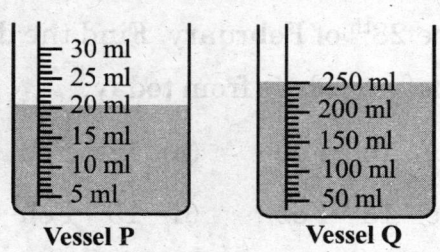

Vessel P   Vessel Q

If the water in vessels P and Q is completely poured into a third vessel R, how many litres of water will there be in vessel R?

(a) 0.02 litre   (b) 0.18 litre
(c) 0.27 litre   (d) 20 litres

31. Sridhar is trying to find a long straight branch to break into three equal places to use it as cricket stumps. A branch of which of these lengths would be most suitable for Sridhar to use?

(a) 210 cm   (b) 210 mm
(c) 21 cm   (d) 21 m

32. Mary went to vegetable market to purchase some vegetables. She purchased 2 kg of potato at the rate of ₹ 10.5 per kg, 3 kg onion at the rate of ₹ 25.50 per kg, 1 kg tomato at the rate of ₹ 34.75 per kg. Find the amount she had spend on marketing.

(a) ₹ 132.25   (b) ₹ 101.75
(c) ₹ 125.75   (d) ₹ 105.75

33. Given map is showing the distances between Rehaan's house,

his school and shopping mall. Which of the following statements is CORRECT?

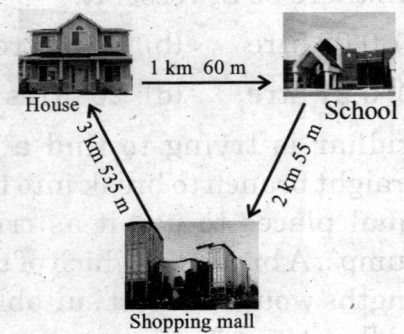

(a) The distance between Rehaan's house and his school is 1600 m.
(b) The distance between Rehaan's house and his school is greater than the distance between his school and the shopping mall.
(c) The distance between the shopping mall and Rehaan's house is 3535 m.
(d) The distance between the shopping mall and Rehaan's house is shorter than the distance between his school and the shopping mall.

34. Veena wanted to take the bus at 5 : 10 p.m. She arrived at the bus stop 25 minutes before 5 : 10 p.m. What time did Veena arrive at the bus stop?

(a) 5 : 35 p.m. (b) 4 : 45 p.m.
(c) 4 : 40 p.m. (d) 4 : 25 p.m.

35. The value of 5 + 5.01 + 51.051 + 515.515 is

(a) 576.567 (b) 567.567
(c) 576.576 (d) 567.576

36. The date on 10th day from today will be 28th of February. Find the date before 6 days from today.

(a) 10th Feb (b) 12th Feb
(c) 13th Feb (d) 15th Feb

———————— *Space for Rough Work* ————————

Mock Test-4 M-33

DIRECTIONS (Qs. 37 & 38): Refer the given table and pictograph which show the number of government employees in some towns.

Name of Town	Number of Govt. Employees
Delhi	4200
Mumbai	5400
Chennai	3000

Name of Town	Number of Govt. Employees
Delhi	▢▢▢▢▢▢▢
Chennai	▢▢▢▢▢

37. How many employees ▢ represent?
    (a) 500   (b) 600
    (c) 700   (d) 800

38. Which of the following is the correct representation of the number of employees in Mumbai?
    (a) ▢▢▢▢
    (b) ▢▢▢▢▢▢
    (c) ▢▢▢▢▢▢▢
    (d) ▢▢▢▢▢

DIRECTION (Q. 39): Find the figure from the alternative which will continue the series given in the problem set.

39.

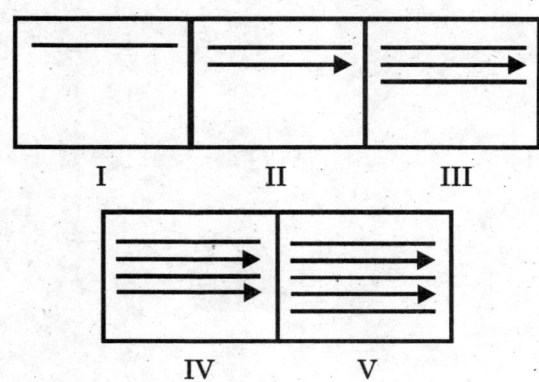

Space for Rough Work

(a)

(b)

(c)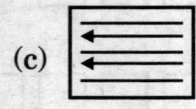

(d)

40.
is same as _____
(a) 121221222
(b) 121121112
(c) 1221112222111122222
(d) None of these

Space for Rough Work

OLYMPIAD Mock Test 5

Name: _____
Number of Questions : 40

Max. Marks : 40
Time : 2 Hours

There is no negative marking in the test.

1. Three-fifth of 15 is denominator and two-fourth of 16 is numerator of a fraction. Find the fraction.
   (a) $\frac{8}{7}$
   (b) $\frac{8}{9}$
   (c) $\frac{9}{8}$
   (d) $\frac{9}{16}$

2. Sum of all the factors of a prime number is
   (a) 1 more than the prime number.
   (b) 1 less than the prime number.
   (c) Equal to the prime number.
   (d) All of these

3. If 3x means 1 × 2 × 3, thus 3x = 6 and if 4x means 1 × 2 × 3 × 4, thus 4x = 24, then 6x is equal to
   (a) 120
   (b) 384
   (c) 720
   (d) 1008

4. The smallest number that should be added to 4321 to get a number divisible by 2 is
   (a) 1
   (b) 2
   (c) 3
   (d) 4

5. The expanded form of 987.564 is
   (a) $9 \times 100 + 8 \times 100 + 7 + \frac{5}{10} + \frac{6}{100} + \frac{4}{1000}$
   (b) $9 \times 100 + 8 \times 10 + 7 + \frac{5}{10} + \frac{6}{100} + \frac{4}{10000}$
   (c) $9 \times 100 + 8 \times 10 + 7 + \frac{5}{10} + \frac{6}{100} + \frac{4}{1000}$
   (d) $9 \times 100 + 8 + \frac{5}{10} + \frac{6}{1000} + \frac{4}{10000}$

6. Which is the smallest?
   (a) 27.027
   (b) 207.27
   (c) 270.27
   (d) 27.27

———— Space for Rough Work ————

7. Arrange the fractions $\frac{1}{2}, \frac{2}{5}, \frac{3}{4}, \frac{4}{7}$ in ascending order.

   (a) $\frac{1}{2} < \frac{2}{5} < \frac{3}{4} < \frac{4}{7}$
   (b) $\frac{2}{5} < \frac{1}{2} < \frac{4}{7} < \frac{3}{4}$
   (c) $\frac{4}{7} < \frac{2}{5} < \frac{3}{4} < \frac{1}{2}$
   (d) $\frac{1}{2} < \frac{4}{7} < \frac{3}{4} < \frac{2}{5}$

8. Which one of the following is a greatest?

   (a) $4\frac{3}{11}$
   (b) $\frac{11}{35}$
   (c) $\frac{7}{4}$
   (d) $\frac{3}{9}$

9. Solve the following question and write the result in Roman Numerals: $55 \div 11 \times 17 - 78 + 32$.
   (a) XXX
   (b) XXVII
   (c) XXXVIII
   (d) XXXIX

10. The value of $0.6 + 7.09 - 3.002$ is
    (a) 4.13
    (b) 3.95
    (c) 4.688
    (d) 4.67

DIRECTIONS (Qs. 11 & 12): This is the score card of a cricket match between India and Australia. Study it carefully and answer questions.

Batsman	Caught and bowled	Runs score	Balls
V. Sehwag	C. Hayden B. Bracken	0	2
Sachin	C. Christ B. Bracken	100	119
V.V.S Laxman	Runout	102	133
Yuvaraj	C. Symonds B. Bracken	44	33
Agarkar	C. Symonds B. Bracken	22	10
Kaif	Not Out	1	1
Extras		15	
Total	284/5 in 50 overs	284	

11. Who was the top scorer in the Indian batting line up?
    (a) Sachin Tendulkar
    (b) V.V.S Laxman
    (c) Yuvaraj Singh
    (d) Ajit Agarkar

12. What was the total number of balls faced by Sachin, Laxman, Yuvaraj and Agarkar?
    (a) 246
    (b) 275
    (c) 295
    (d) 300

13. Consider the following statements.
    Statement 1: There are 300 tens in 3 hundreds.
    Statement 2: Face value of a digit in a number is the digit itself.
    Now, choose the correct option.
    (a) Statement 1 is true and 2 is false.
    (b) Statement 1 is false and 2 is true.

(c) Both statements are true.
(d) Both statements are false.

14. If the cost of 1 packet of TIGER biscuits is ₹ 5, how many packets can I get for ₹ 30 with the FREE OFFER shown here?

free! free! free!
with every 2 packets of TIGER biscuits, get 1 packet absolutely free

(a) 6 (b) 9
(c) 10 (d) 12

15. Each letter A to F stands for the given digits respectively.

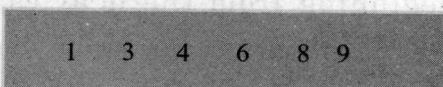

| 1 | 3 | 4 | 6 | 8 | 9 |

Then, the value of (F × B) = ?
(a) (C × D) + E
(b) (C × C) + F
(c) (C × D) + B
(d) D × E

16. Two numbers which have no other common factor except 1 are called _____ numbers.
(a) prime
(b) co-prime
(c) composite
(d) twin prime

17. The product of even numbers between 1 and 9 is
(a) 386 (b) 380
(c) 382 (d) 384

18. Find the angles from the options given below which represents a quadrilateral.
(a) (80°, 150°, 90°, 70°)
(b) (80°, 150°, 60°, 80°)
(c) (70°, 160°, 50°, 90°)
(d) (90°, 120°, 80°, 70°)

19. Match the following columns.

	Column -I	Column-II
A.	$\dfrac{9}{14} - \dfrac{5}{14}$	1. $1\dfrac{4}{35}$
B.	$\dfrac{2}{5} + \dfrac{5}{7}$	2. $4\dfrac{5}{7}$
C.	$5 - \dfrac{2}{7}$	3. $\dfrac{2}{7}$
D.	$3 + \dfrac{3}{7}$	4. $3\dfrac{3}{7}$

	A	B	C	D
(a)	1	3	4	2
(b)	3	1	2	4
(c)	1	2	3	4
(d)	3	2	1	4

―――――― *Space for Rough Work* ――――――

20. The number of vertices of a cuboid is
 (a) 6   (b) 8
 (c) 12 (d) 18

21. The value of 22222 − 2222 + 222 − 22 + 2 is
 (a) 20220 (b) 22022
 (c) 20202 (d) 22020

22. In which of the following figures dotted lines shows a line of symmetry?

 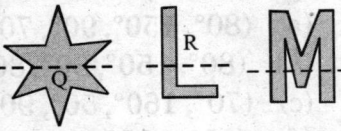

 (a) P   (b) Q
 (c) R   (d) S

23. Which of the following set has equivalent fractions?
 (a) $\frac{1}{2}, \frac{1}{3}, \frac{1}{4}, \frac{1}{5}$ (b) $\frac{2}{7}, \frac{3}{7}, \frac{4}{7}, \frac{5}{7}$
 (c) $\frac{2}{3}, \frac{8}{12}, \frac{6}{9}, \frac{4}{6}$ (d) None of these

24. The smallest 5-digit number formed by using the digits 2, 0, 3, 6, 5 is
 (a) 02356
 (b) 20356
 (c) 30256
 (d) 65320

25. A playground which is 250 m long and 20 m broad is to be fenced with wire. How much wire is needed?
 (a) 270 m
 (b) 230 m
 (c) 540 m
 (d) None of these

26. Priya wants to visit her daughter living in New York in a hostel which is 345 km 255 m from her residence. Due to some work, she will have to first visit her sister who is living at a distance of 69 km from her residence and then she will go to see her daughter. If New York is at a distance of 389 km 540 m from her sister's residence, then find the extra distance she will have to travel.
 (a) 112 km 265 m
 (b) 145 km 772 m
 (c) 113 km 285 m
 (d) 172 km 228 m

27. Arrange the boxes in order, beginning from the heaviest to lightest.

 (a) P, Q, R, S   (b) Q, R, S, P
 (c) R, P, S, Q   (d) S, Q, R, P

28. The capacity of a small container is 380 ml and the capacity of a big

Space for Rough Work

container is 1250 ml. If Aakash uses 8 small containers and 1 big container of water to fill up an empty tank, then what is the capacity of the tank?
(a) 3750 ml (b) 4290 ml
(c) 3040 ml (d) 4190 ml

29. Which of the following figures has exactly 3 lines of symmetry?

(a) 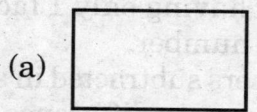   (b)

(c) 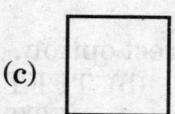   (d)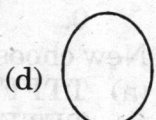

30. If five days before today was Sunday, then what will be the day after 7 day from today?
(a) Tuesday (b) Wednesday
(c) Thursday (d) Friday

31. Find the difference between the time of two clocks as shown below in seconds.

(a) 620 sec   (b) 580 sec

(c) 600 sec   (d) 590 sec

32. The number of weeks in 147 days are
(a) 27 (b) 21
(c) 23 (d) 22

33. How many days were there in February 2003?
(a) 27 (b) 28
(c) 29 (d) 30

34.

What is the time shown on the digital clock?
(a) A quarter past one in the afternoon.
(b) A quarter to one in the afternoon.
(c) One fifty in the afternoon.
(d) One fifteen in the morning.

35. Pandu, Ravi, Bijji and Raghu are friends. They all collect toy cars. This graph shows how many toy cars each of them have.

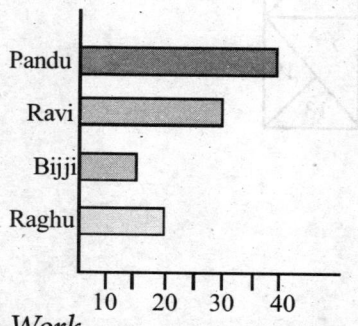

What can we conclude from the above graph?
(a) Bijji has one-third the number of cars Pandu has.
(b) Three children have more than 20 cars.
(c) Ravi has twice as many cars as Bijji.
(d) Bijji has 1 car less than Raghu.

36. If 3# represents 3 + 2 + 1 and 3* represents 3 − 2 then the value of (6#) × (4*) is
(a) 42 (b) 32
(c) 21 (d) 2

37. The movie tickets of 8 people cost ₹ 1000. What will be the cost of 24 tickets?
(a) ₹ 300 (b) ₹ 5000
(c) ₹ 3000 (d) ₹ 4500

38. Find the missing term from the figure shown below.

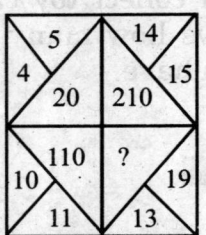

(a) 227 (b) 236
(c) 247 (d) 249

39. The product of XXIX and XXXI is
(a) 651 (b) 899
(c) 989 (d) 1131

40. Consider the following statements.
A : A number having more than two factors is a composite number.
B : A number having only 1 factor is a prime number.
C : Two numbers subtracted in any order gives same difference.
D : 0 multiplied to a number gives 0.
New choose the correct option.
(a) TTFF (b) TFFT
(c) TFTF (d) FFTT

SCIENCE MOCK TEST 1-5

OLYMPIAD Mock Test 1

Name : _____
Number of Questions : 40
Max. Marks : 40
Time : 2 Hours

There is no negative marking in the test.

1. Which of the following is are characteristic(s) of all living organisms?
   (a) Reproduction
   (b) Movement
   (c) Respiration
   (d) Both (a) & (c)

2. Which of the following would be classified as a 'living' organism?
   (a) Volcano   (b) Cloud
   (c) Virus   (d) Bacteria

3. Match the following and select the correct answer.

List-I	List-II
A. Ginger	1. Leaf
B. Radish	2. Seed
C. Spinach	3. Root
D. Rice	4. Stem

   (a) A-1, B-4, C-2, D-3
   (b) A-4, B-3, C-1, D-2
   (c) A-1, B-2, C-3, D-4
   (d) A-3, B-2, C-4, D-1

4. During photosynthesis, plants use _____ gas and release _____ gas.
   (a) carbon dioxide, oxygen
   (b) oxygen, carbon dioxide
   (c) oxygen, nitrogen
   (d) nitrogen, oxygen

5. Which of the following is ectoparasite ?
   (a) Roundworm
   (b) Tapworm
   (c) Hookworm
   (d) Leech

_____ Space for Rough Work _____

6. Match the animals given in Column 'A' to their young ones given in Column 'B'.

Column A	Column B
A. Butterfly	1. Fry
B. Frog	2. Nymph
C. Fish	3. Larva
D. Cockroach	4. Tadpole

   (a) A-1, B-2, C-3, D-4
   (b) A-3, B-4, C-1, D-2
   (c) A-2, B-3, C-4, D-1
   (d) A-4, B-3, C-2, D-1

7. Which of the following stages in life cycles is in correct order?
   (a) Baby → teenager → child → adult
   (b) Seed → flower → plant → fruit
   (c) Cocoon → larva → egg → adult
   (d) Egg → caterpillar → pupa → butterfly

8. Which of the following correctly represents the passage of oxygen in the respiratory system?
   (a) Nose → Lungs → Windpipe → Blood
   (b) Nose → Blood → Windpipe → Lungs
   (c) Nose → Blood → Lungs → Windpipe
   (d) Nose → Windpipe → Lungs → Blood

9. Match the internal organs shown in the figure with their respective names.

P	Q	R	S

   (a) P- Heart, Q-Lungs, R-Kidney, S-Stomach
   (b) P-Lungs, Q-Kidney, R-Stomach, S-Heart
   (c) P-Heart, Q-Lungs, R-Stomach, S-Kidney
   (d) P-Heart, Q-Kidney, R-Lungs, S-Stomach

10. Mr. Kim touches a hot metal and spontaneously withdraws his hand from the metal. Why does he react spontaneously?
    (a) He wants to maintain the temperature of his hand.
    (b) He is shocked by the hot metal.
    (c) His body shows reflex action towards the high temperature.
    (d) He is under pressure.

―――――――――― Space for Rough Work ――――――――――

Mock Test-1

11. Which of the following food components are needed in small quantities?
    (a) Proteins
    (b) Vitamins
    (c) Fats
    (d) Carbohydrates

12. How does digestion take place in the small intestine?
    (a) By storing of food.
    (b) By the release of juices.
    (c) By cutting of food.
    (d) By absorption of food.

13. A runner participating in a race takes some glucose just before the race begins. This means that glucose
    (a) Makes breathing easier.
    (b) Builds muscles instantly.
    (c) Gives energy instantly.
    (d) Stops sweating of the body.

14. The teeth that are well-developed in carnivores are
    (a) Incisors   (b) Canines
    (c) Premolars   (d) Molars

15. This picture shows:
    (a) A canine tooth
    (b) An incisor tooth
    (c) A premolar tooth
    (d) A molar tooth

16. Which gas is mainly responsible for the global warming?
    (a) Methane
    (b) Nitrogen
    (c) Carbon dioxide
    (d) Oxygen

17. By recycling,
    (a) We can make useful things from waste materials.
    (b) We can save natural resources.
    (c) We can control pollution.
    (d) All of these.

18. Observe the chart given below.

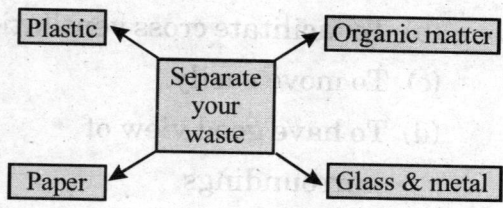

Which of these cannot be recycled?
    (a) Plastic
    (b) Paper
    (c) Glass & metal
    (d) Organic matter

Space for Rough Work

19. Which of the following statements is not true?
    (a) Igloos are found in places where it rains throughout the year.
    (b) Tents protect nomads from heat and dust storm.
    (c) Animals and birds also have shelters.
    (d) Sheds and stables must be kept clean everyday.
20. The windows should be in opposite direction to the door so that
    (a) More light enters the house.
    (b) To facilitate cross ventilation.
    (c) To move easily.
    (d) To have good view of surroundings.
21. Which of the following statements are correct?
    (a) The condition of the atmosphere is known as weather.
    (b) Average weather conditions at a place are known as climate.
    (c) When a particular weather continues for months, it is a season.
    (d) All of these.
22. In which place would the weather remain almost the same whole year?
    (a) On a hill station.
    (b) Near the coast.
    (c) Near a desert.
    (d) Near a river.
23. Deforestation will cause
    i. Soil erosion.
    ii. Depletion of water catchment areas.
    iii. Global warming
    (a) i and ii only (b) i and iii only
    (c) ii and iii only (d) i, ii and iii
24. Most of the metals are found
    (a) in the wood of trees.
    (b) on the top of mountains.
    (c) deep inside the earth.
    (d) dissolved in water.

25. Different amount of air with different pressures are in balloons of the same material and size. Which of them will be the easiest to prick?

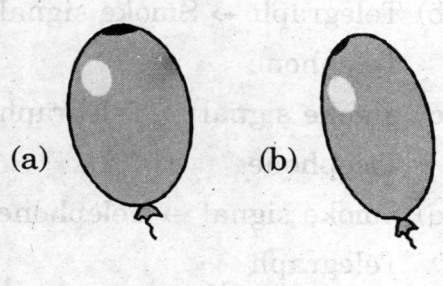

26. Which of the following conversions is correct?
    (a) Water —heat→ Steam —heat→ Ice
    (b) Steam —cool→ Water —cool→ Ice
    (c) Water —cool→ Ice —cool→ Steam
    (d) Steam —heat→ Ice —cool→ Water

27. A football kicked by a boy rolls on the ground to some distance and stops. The force which stops the ball is
    (a) Muscular force
    (b) Gravitational force
    (c) Mechanical force
    (d) Frictional force

28. The following diagram shows a boy pushing a table. The boy is applying _____ on the table.
    (a) work
    (b) force
    (c) energy
    (d) muscles

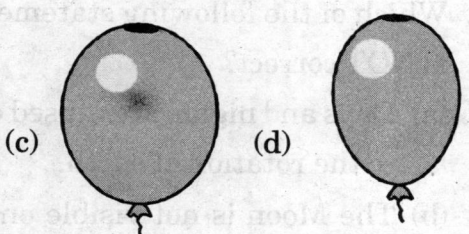

29. Manoj wants to find out how hot or cold a glass of milk is. He should use a _____ to check.
    (a) metre rod
    (b) weighing machine
    (c) stop watch
    (d) thermometer

———————— Space for Rough Work ————————

30. The nearest star to the earth is
    (a) Sirius
    (b) Alpha Centauri
    (c) Moon
    (d) Pole Star
31. Which of the following does not represent advanced method in communication technology?
    (a) Cell phone
    (b) Computer
    (c) DTH (Direct to Home) dish antenna
    (d) A microwave oven
32. Which of the following is a disadvantage caused by development of technology?
    (a) Technology saves time.
    (b) Work can be easily done by technology.
    (c) Technology improves quality of life.
    (d) Technology has resulted in increasing atmospheric pollution.
33. Which of the following orders of development of technology in communication is correct?
    (a) Telephone → Telegraph → Smoke signal
    (b) Telegraph → Smoke signal → Telephone
    (c) Smoke signal → Telegraph → Telephone
    (d) Smoke signal → Telephone → Telegraph
34. Which of the following statements is NOT correct?
    (a) Days and nights are caused due to the rotation of earth.
    (b) The Moon is not visible on all nights.
    (c) Earth takes 365 days to complete one revolution.
    (d) Moon takes 365 Earth days to complete one revolution around the sun.

─────────────── Space for Rough Work ───────────────

35. Mercury can be seen only in the morning and evening because
    (a) it is very close to the Sun.
    (b) it is very small.
    (c) it is very hot.
    (d) it does not have any light of its own

36. Which of the following animals breathe through the gills?
    (a) Tadpole   (b) Fish
    (c) Both a & b   (d) Crab

37. We call an animal that hunts for its food as a
    (a) Carnivore   (b) Consumer
    (c) Predator   (d) Scavenger

38. Which of the following activities is an example of telecommunication?
    (a) Using the internet to send messages
    (b) Playing computer games
    (c) Typing on a computer
    (d) Listening to songs

39. The excretory system works to remove wastes from the body. The body produces liquid, solid and gaseous wastes. Which organ is responsible for eliminating liquid waste?
    (a) Lungs
    (b) Heart
    (c) Kidneys
    (d) Small intestine

40. At which age, 90% of weight of brain is achieved?
    (a) 2 years   (b) 4 years
    (c) 5 years   (d) 6 years

Space for Rough Work

OLYMPIAD Mock Test 2

Name : _____
Number of Questions : 40

Max. Marks : 40
Time : 2 Hours

There is no negative marking in the test.

1. Which of the following is a characteristic feature of living things?
   (a) Living things do not reproduce.
   (b) Living things do not need air.
   (c) Living things do not grow.
   (d) Living things respond to their environment.

2. What do you abserve when you plant rocks and seeds?
   (a) When we plant rocks and seeds, only the seeds grow.
   (b) When we plant rocks and seeds both rocks and seeds grow.
   (c) Rocks need sunlight to grow.
   (d) When we plant rocks and seeds, only the rocks grow.

3. An electric heater is an example of _____.
   (a) heat energy
   (b) electrical energy
   (c) gravitatunal energy
   (d) muscular energy

4. Which of the following animals make their own home?
   (a) Pigeon   (b) Tiger
   (c) Lion   (d) Cuckoo

5. In radish, food is stored in
   (a) Leaves   (b) Stem
   (c) Roots   (d) Flowers

6. Cactus is a desert plant. To minimise loss of water it does not have leaves. The stem is green and waxy and prepares food for the plant. This shows that

———— *Space for Rough Work* ————

(a) Habitat changes according to plants.
(b) Plants modify themselves according to their habitats.
(c) Cactus is insectivorous in nature.
(d) Wax is obtained from cactus.

7. The eggs of fish are called
   (a) Larva   (b) Pupa
   (c) Spawn   (d) Cocoon

8. I. Snakes   II. Cats
   III. Birds   IV. Frogs
   Which of the above animals reproduce by laying eggs?
   (a) I and III only
   (b) I and IV only
   (c) II and IV only
   (d) I, III and IV only

9. The method by which animals blend with the surrounding and protects them from predators is known as _____.
   (a) hibernation
   (b) aestivation
   (c) camouflage
   (d) none of these

10. What is soil fertility?
    (a) The amount of nutrients in soil
    (b) The composition of soil
    (c) The type of soil
    (d) All of these

11. Which of the following systems is responsible for controlling all the activities in the human body?
    (a) Excretory system
    (b) Circulatory system
    (c) Respiratory system
    (d) Nervous system

12. In the figure given below, urine is stored in

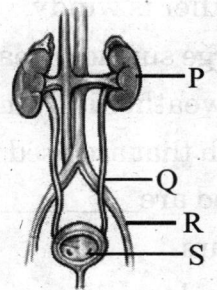

    (a) P   (b) Q
    (c) R   (d) S

--- Space for Rough Work ---

13. Which of the following is a rich source of protein?
    (a) Wheat
    (b) Pulses
    (c) Meat
    (d) Both (b) and (c)

14. Which of the following can be prepared in our body with the help of sunlight?
    (a) Vitamin A
    (b) Vitamin B
    (c) Vitamin D
    (d) Vitamin C

15. Water evaporates slowly when the:
    (a) weather is hot.
    (b) weather is windy.
    (c) a large surface area is exposed.
    (d) the weather is humid.

16. The teeth that are used for cracking hard food are _____.
    (a) molars
    (b) premolars
    (c) canines
    (d) incisors

17. In the diagram given below, the teeth marked 'X' are called:
    (a) Molars
    (b) Premolars
    (c) Incisors
    (d) Canines

18. Which of the following is not a natural source of water?
    (a) River
    (b) Lakes
    (c) Stream
    (d) Dams

19. Which of the following diseases is caused because of unclean surroundings and bad food habits?
    (a) Cancer
    (b) AIDS
    (c) Small Pox
    (d) Diarrhoea

20. Germs present in water can be killed by
    (a) Boiling
    (b) Decantation
    (c) Filtration
    (d) Condensation

21. Minu and her friends went on a picnic and threw banana peels on the beach. Which one of these is the reason that this should not be done?
    (a) Banana peels do not mix with the soil for number of years.
    (b) Banana peels make the beach unhygienic and dirty.
    (c) Banana peels are harmful to animals on the beach that eat them.
    (d) Banana peels pollute the water because they contain harmful chemicals.
22. In the areas having high rain and snow fall, the houses have
    (a) flat roofs
    (b) circular roofs
    (c) sloping roofs
    (d) rectangular roofs
23. Which of these does not belong to the group formed by others?
    (a) Cement   (b) Brick
    (c) Iron   (d) Straw
24. Ghee in winter solidifies. When it is kept on burning stove it liquifies again. This type of change is
    (a) No change
    (b) Chemical change
    (c) Physical change
    (d) Both b and c
25. Water droplets that can be seen on grass in winter mornings is because of
    (a) the secretion of water from the leaves.
    (b) rains that take place every night.
    (c) condensation of water particles in the air.
    (d) excessive absorption of water from the soil.
26. Which of the following activities require the presence of air?
    (a) Burning of wood
    (b) Respiration
    (c) Flying of aeroplane
    (d) All of these

Space for Rough Work

27. Animal dung and rotten vegetables can be used
    (a) as insecticides.
    (b) as manure.
    (c) in making bricks.
    (d) to make oil.

28. Garden soil is most suitable for plant growth because
    (a) it contains humus which makes the soil fertile.
    (b) it holds enough water for plants to grow.
    (c) its loose soil texture contains air.
    (d) all of these

29. Which of the following transformations is occurring in the given figure?

    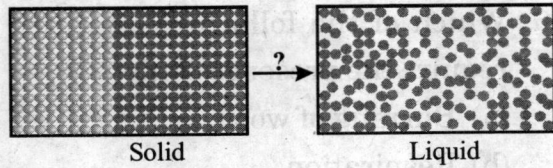
    Solid   Liquid

    (a) Condensation   (b) Melting
    (c) Evaporation   (d) Boiling

30. Which of the following is NOT an outcome of condensation?
    (a) Hail
    (b) Fog
    (c) Air currents
    (d) Frost

31. If we take three samples of a soild, liquid and gas, each having a fixed volume of $1 cm^3$, then which of them will have the most number of molecules?
    (a) Solid
    (b) Liquid
    (c) Gas
    (d) It will be same in all the three

32. A goal keeper stopped a moving ball by applying force. What inference can you draw from this example?
    (a) The ball was slow.
    (b) Force can change the shape of an obect.
    (c) Force can stop a moving object.
    (d) The ball stopped due to frictional force.

———————— *Space for Rough Work* ————————

33. The least measurement that can be done accurately by using a standard scale is
    (a) 1 metre
    (b) 1 centimetre
    (c) 1 millimetre
    (d) 1 kilometre
34. Which of these can be used to measure the length of a curved wire?
    (a) A ruler
    (b) A thread
    (c) A thread and a ruler
    (d) A measuring jar
35. Your teacher has asked you to measure the length of one side of your classroom. Which of the following will you use to measure it?
    (a) Measuring cylinder
    (b) Measuring tape
    (c) Ruler
    (d) None of these
36. Which of the following is not a part of the solar system?
    (a) Earth
    (b) Moon
    (c) Jupiter
    (d) Pole star
37. The sizes of the Sun, the Earth and the Moon arranged in ascending order is
    (a) Sun, Moon, Earth
    (b) Sun, Earth, Moon
    (c) Moon, Earth, Sun
    (d) Moon, Sun, Earth
38. Cactus and camel live in this habitat.
    (a) Ocean
    (b) Rain forest
    (c) Desert
    (d) Polar region

39. Match the following and select the correct answer.

A. 		1.	Saliva mixes with food
B. 		2.	Absorption of food takes place
C.		3.	Secrete bile juice
D.		4.	Churning of food takes place

(a) A-4, B-3, C-2, D-1 (b) A-3, B-4, C-2, D-1
(c) A-2, B-1, C-3, D-4 (d) A-1, B-4, C-3, D-2

40. Match the following and select the correct answer.
   A. Kidney   1. Control and coordination
   B. Brain   2. Sense of hearing
   C. Tongue   3. Nitrogenous waste
   D. Ear   4. Taste buds
   (a) A-1, B-2, C-3, D-4   (b) A-2, B-3, C-4, D-1
   (c) A-2, B-4, C-1, D-3   (d) A-3, B-1, C-4, D-2

OLYMPIAD Mock Test 3

Name : _____ **Max. Marks : 35**
Number of Questions : 35 **Time : 2 Hours**

There is no negative marking in the test.

1. The small organisms, which cause diseases are called ___.
   (a) pathogens
   (b) pesticides
   (c) microbes
   (d) insecticides

2. Growing of canine teeth and strong claws in carnivorous animals is an adaptation ____.
   (a) that easily suits the climatic condition
   (b) to catch and kill its prey
   (c) for chewing the flesh
   (d) both (b) and (c)

3. Name the biggest natural satellite of the planet Saturn.
   (a) Moon
   (b) Ganymede
   (c) Europa
   (d) Titan

4. Which one of the following is a mammal?

5. The force by which earth attracts moon is _____.
   (a) frictional force
   (b) mechanical force
   (c) gravitational force
   (d) magnetic force

―――――――――― *Space for Rough Work* ――――――――――

6. Which one of the following is a fossil fuel?
   (a) Wind   (b) Water
   (c) Sunlight   (d) Petroleum

7. Which one of the following is the correct description for reflection of light?
   (a) Sending back the coming light by an object.
   (b) Change in the direction of coming light.
   (c) Change in the speed of coming light.
   (d) Entering of light from one medium to another medium.

8. Galaxies have been classified into three groups according to their shape. Look at the shape of given galaxy carefully and identify what kind of galaxy is this?

   (a) Spiral
   (b) Elliptical
   (c) Irregular
   (d) All of these

9. Which one of the following gasses is essential for the process of burning?
   (a) Carbon dioxide
   (b) Hydrogen
   (c) Oxygen
   (d) Methane

10. When a solid substance is changed into gas without coming into liquid state, the process is called_____.
    (a) evaporation
    (b) vaporization
    (c) sublimation
    (d) condensation

11. When the same amount of force is applied on two different surfaces, the surface having greater area will produce ____ pressure.
    (a) less
    (b) more
    (c) same
    (d) all of these

———— Space for Rough Work ————

12. Which one of the following instruments converts chemical energy into mechanical energy?
    (a) Bus   (b) Bull
    (c) TV   (d) Radio
13. In which one of the following layers of atmosphere, the layer of ozone is present?

    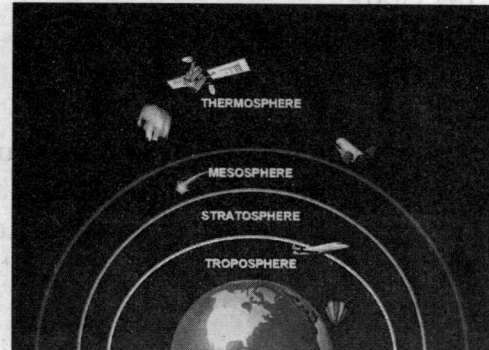

    (a) Troposphere
    (b) Stratosphere
    (c) Mesosphere
    (d) Thermosphere
14. Identify the hardest part of the human body.
    (a) Dentine   (b) Enamel
    (c) Pulp   (d) Gums
15. In which one of the following states of matter, intermolecular force is least?
    (a) Solid
    (b) Liquid
    (c) Gas
    (d) In all states of matter, intermolecular force remains same.
16. When water starts boiling, bubbles are formed. Which one of the following reasons is responsible for this?
    (a) These bubbles are actually dissolved gases which separate from water on heating.
    (b) These bubbles are nothing just water droplets which keep on changing into gas.
    (c) These bubbles are water vapours which are formed due to boiling of water.
    (d) All of these

17. A substance is in solid state. If we heat the substance, the force between the molecules gets____.
    (a) stronger
    (b) weaker
    (c) remains same, independent of heat
    (d) reduced to zero
18. Which one of the following planets is the second largest planet of our solar system?
    (a) Jupiter   (b) Saturn
    (c) Mars   (d) Neptune
19. Which one of the following are biodegradable substances?
    (a) Wood
    (b) Dead plants
    (c) Dead animals
    (d) All of these
20. Which one of the following is a carnivorous animal?

    (a)    (b)

    (c)    (d)

21. Which one of the following is a chemical change?
    (a) Bursting of tyre
    (b) Turning milk sour
    (c) Breaking up of stones
    (d) Falling of an object from a height
22. Which one of the following is a metamorphic rock?
    (a) Slate
    (b) Limestone
    (c) Shale
    (d) Granite
23. The two objects of same mass are moving with different speed. The object which has greater speed, has possessed____ amount of kinetic energy.
    (a) greater
    (b) smaller
    (c) same
    (d) all of these
24. Observe the following figure carefully. Select the correct option.

Space for Rough Work

(a) It is polluting the environment therefore it is not good.
(b) It is cleaning the environment therefore it is good.
(c) It has nothing to do with the environment.
(d) All of these

25. While walking on the road you step on an object (plastic bottle) and crush it. The shape of the object is changed. What kind of change takes place in the object?
(a) Chemical change
(b) Physical change
(c) Both chemical and physical change
(d) Partially physical and partially chemical

26. Which one of the following is the biotic component of the environment?
(a) Plastics
(b) Microorganisms
(c) Air
(d) Water

27. While playing in the ground, Steve strikes a football with greater force and the ball hits another ball in the way. What kind of energy is transferred by the ball kicked by Steve to another ball?
(a) Potential (b) Kinetic
(c) Mechanical (d) Light

28. Which one of the following pollutions is called hydrospheric pollution?
(a) Land Pollution
(b) Water Pollution
(c) Soil Pollution
(d) Air Pollution

29. When something delicious is cooked in our kitchen, we smell it and can imagine its taste. How is it possible?
(a) Sense of smell and taste are linked.
(b) Nose and tongue are close to each other.
(c) Smell itself shows taste.
(d) All of these

Space for Rough Work

30. What kind of force does the stretched rubber band has?
    (a) Balanced force
    (b) Unbalanced force
    (c) Tension force
    (d) Air resistance force
31. Rocks are the chief source of the parent material from which soils are developed. The main kind of rocks which play an important role in the formation of soils are ____.
    (a) igneous rocks
    (b) sedimentary rocks
    (c) metamorphic rocks
    (d) all of these
32. Which type of force is weak, but very long ranged. Furthermore, it is always attractive, and acts between any two pieces of matter in the universe?
    (a) Electromagnetic force
    (b) Gravitational force
    (c) Weak force
    (d) Strong force
33. Kidney removes waste products from our body. What are the waste products that are removed by kidney?
    (a) Urea and water
    (b) Carbon dioxide and water
    (c) Urea and salts
    (d) Urea, water and salts
34. Which type of joint permits a wide range, mostly sideways movement as well as movement in one direction.
    (a) Ball-and-Socket Joint
    (b) Hinge Joint
    (c) Gliding Joint
    (d) Saddle Joint
35. Match the following.

List-I		List-II
A. Exists in all the three states	1.	Physical change
B. Changing of ice into water	2.	Water
C. Basic unit of matter	3.	Molecule
D. Smallest particle that exist independently	4.	Atom

    (a) A-1, B-3, C-2, D-4
    (b) A-2, B-1, C-4, D-3
    (c) A-1, B-3, C-4, D-2
    (d) A-3, B-1, C-2, D-4

OLYMPIAD Mock Test 4

Name : _____
Number of Questions : 35
There is no negative marking in the test.

Max. Marks : 35
Time : 2 Hours

1. Brain is protected by a bony structure called _____.
   (a) rib cage   (b) skull
   (c) spinal chord (d) bladder

2. If an object is placed at greater height, the potential energy of the object is _____.
   (a) increased   (b) decreased
   (c) same   (d) all of these

3. When one atom of oxygen and two atoms of hydrogen are combined together, one molecule of water is formed. This type of change is _____.
   (a) physical change
   (b) chemical change
   (c) biological change
   (d) Both (a) and (b)

4. Who between the following two friends is correct ?
   Rahul: Biodegradable substances are the main cause of land pollution.
   Aman: Non-biodegradable substances play important role in polluting the soil as they do not get easily degraded.
   (a) Rahul
   (b) Aman
   (c) Both are correct
   (d) Both are incorrect

5. Hibernation is a process in which an animal goes for winter sleep. What is the reason behind this?
   (a) Due to tiredness
   (b) Due to scarcity of food and extreme cold
   (c) To compensate the consumed energy
   (d) To digest the food

───────── *Space for Rough Work* ─────────

6. Name the animal which is also known as "Touch-me-not".
   (a) Lion (b) Fish
   (c) Porcupine (d) Rat

7. Some organisms go through several changes before being an adult, this process is called metamorphosis. In which one of the following options, different stages of metamorphosis has been correctly arranged for a butterfly?
   (a) Egg - pupa - caterpiller - adult butterfly
   (b) Egg - caterpiller - pupa - adult butterfly
   (c) Pupa - egg - caterpiller - adult butterfly
   (d) Pupa - caterpiller - egg - adult butterfly

8. When we put a piece of wood in the water, it floats and does not sink. Which one of the following forces is responsible for this?
   (a) Frictional force
   (b) Gravitational force
   (c) Upthrust force
   (d) Magnetic force

9. Sometimes in the sky we see a string of light for a moment. Actually these are meteors which burn on entering into the atmosphere of the Earth. Which one of the following gives the required heat energy to the meteors to be burnt?
   (a) Friction
   (b) Gravitation
   (c) Upthrust
   (d) All of these

10. We measure the potential energy of a body with the help of the formula "m g h". Here 'g' stands for _____ .
    (a) gravitational force
    (b) gravitational acceleration
    (c) gravitational constant
    (d) all of these

11. Belt of asteroids lie between the orbits of the planets _____
    (a) Earth and Mars
    (b) Neptune and Jupiter
    (c) Mars and Jupiter
    (d) Jupiter and Saturn

Space for Rough Work

12. Which one of the following systems is responsible for exchanging the information between body parts and the brain?
    (a) Excretory system
    (b) Respiratory system
    (c) Nervous system
    (d) Circulatory system
13. In the soil which one of the following is most helpful to the growth of the plant?
    (a) Humus   (b) Clay
    (c) Porous rocks (d) Sand
14. Terrace farming or step farming helps in _____ soil erosion.
    (a) reducing
    (b) increasing
    (c) removing
    (d) all of these
15. Malaria is a disease caused by _____.
    (a) virus   (b) bacteria
    (c) ringworm   (d) protozoa
16. Observe the following figure carefully.

    What kind of change are you observing?
    (a) Physical change
    (b) Chemical change
    (c) Biological change
    (d) Both (a) and (b)
17. Which one of the following organs is specialized for filtering water from blood?
    (a) Heart   (b) Lung
    (c) Liver   (d) Kidney
18. When clothes dry in air, which of the following process takes place?
    (a) Evaporation
    (b) Condensation
    (c) Boiling
    (d) Melting

─────────── Space for Rough Work ───────────

19. In the following figure, molecular structure of a substance has been shown. The substance is in _____ state.

    (a) solid
    (b) liquid
    (c) gaseous
    (d) all of these

20. Which one of the following is an invertebrate animal?
    (a) Lion
    (b) Fish
    (c) Rat
    (d) Earthworm

21. Waxy coating on the surface of the leaves of aquatic plants is for
    (a) shining
    (b) preventing rotting
    (c) photosynthesis
    (d) respiration

22. The _____ allows movement of the wrist and ankle.
    (a) gliding joint
    (b) pivot joint
    (c) hinge joint
    (d) ball and socket joint

23. Which kind of food give us strength to fight against disease?
    (a) Carbohydrate rich food
    (b) Fat rich food
    (c) Protein rich food
    (d) Vitamin and mineral rich food

24. Which one of the following forces work only when objects are in contact with each other?
    (a) Magnetic force
    (b) Gravitational force
    (c) Frictional force
    (d) Electrostatic force

25. Name the state that produces the highest amount of electricity using wind energy.
    (a) Gujarat
    (b) Delhi
    (c) Tamil Nadu
    (d) Kerela

26. Green plants make their own food by the process of photosynthesis. In what form does the photosynthesis provide food to the green plants?
    (a) Starch
    (b) Glucose
    (c) Carbohydrate
    (d) All of these

27. You get energy by eating food. This is an example of ____.
    (a) physical change
    (b) chemical change
    (c) nuclear change
    (d) atomic change

28. Which one of the following have no role in digestion of food?
    (a) Liver
    (b) Gall bladder
    (c) Stomach
    (d) Kidney

29. Which one of the following is non-renewable source of energy?
    (a) Tidal energy
    (b) Wind energy
    (c) Solar energy
    (d) Fossil fuels

30. Given below are the features of leaves of plants.
    1. Submerged leaves, are very thin and narrow, often highly dissected and very flexible.
    2. Floating leaves, are broader leaves. They are firm or leathery but flexible enough to resist tearing by wave action.
    Which one of the following plants possess the type of leaves mentioned above?
    (a) Desert plants
    (b) Plants in the hilly areas
    (c) Aquatic plants
    (d) All of these

31. Consider the following two statements:
    Statement A: Energy is the ability to do work.
    Statement B: Potential energy of the object is due to its motion.
    Which of the following is correct with respect to the above statements?
    (a) Statement A is correct.
    (b) Statement B is correct.
    (c) Both Statements A and B are correct.
    (d) Both Statements A and B are incorrect.

―――――――― Space for Rough Work ――――――――

32. Which type of canned milk is made by removing half of the water from whole milk. It is then highly sweetened and as a result this milk has very high calories?
    (a) Sweetened condensed
    (b) Pasteurized
    (c) Homogenized
    (d) Skimmed
33. The earth rotates from _____ .
    (a) west to east
    (b) east to west
    (c) north to south
    (d) south to north
34. You are holding a stone in your hand. What kind of energy does the stone have?
    (a) Potential energy
    (b) Kinetic energy
    (c) rotational energy
    (d) All of these
35. Match the following.

    A. Heart   1. is located between the stomach and the anus.
    B. Stomach   2. are paired organs.
    C. Intestine 3. digests food
    D. Lungs   4. is a hollow, muscular organ.

	A	B	C	D
(a)	2	3	1	4
(b)	4	1	3	2
(c)	4	3	2	1
(d)	4	3	1	2

OLYMPIAD Mock Test 5

Name : _____
Number of Questions : 35
Max. Marks : 35
Time : 2 Hours

There is no negative marking in the test.

1. Nowadays, many _____ travel at a supersonic speed.
   (a) trains
   (b) planes
   (c) ships
   (d) two wheelers

2. When the layer of air that surrounds the earth presses down, this is called _____.
   (a) heat
   (b) temperature
   (c) air pressure
   (d) precipitation

3. The energy an object gets from its motion is
   (a) electrical energy
   (b) chemical energy
   (c) kinetic energy
   (d) potential energy

4. The pull or push of an object is called _____.
   (a) gravity
   (b) friction
   (c) force
   (d) inertia

5. Plants use sunlight to make sugar in the process of
   (a) oxidation
   (b) reproduction
   (c) photosynthesis
   (d) fertilization

6. The nerves that carry the messages from the sense organs to the spinal cord or brain are
   (a) Sensory nerves
   (b) Motor nerves
   (c) All of the above
   (d) None of the above

——————— Space for Rough Work ———————

7. Rubber, glass and plastic are good _____.
   (a) conductors
   (b) generators
   (c) insulators
   (d) electromagnets

8. Study the following Venn diagram carefully. Which letter represents the hen?

   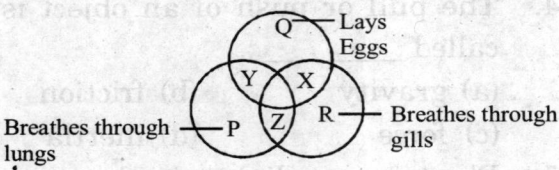

   (a) Y
   (b) X
   (c) Z
   (d) R

9. Which process is occurring at S?

   (a) Condensation
   (b) Evaporation
   (c) Precipitation
   (d) Runoff

10. In which of the following, will the force of attraction between the molecules be highest?
    (a) Water
    (b) Ice
    (c) Steam
    (d) Liquid

11. House in hot and dry regions have _____.
    (a) thick flat roof
    (b) slopping roof
    (c) dome roof
    (d) circular roof

12. The nutrients that protect our body from various diseases and keep us fit and healthy are
    (a) carbohydrate and fat
    (b) proteins and vitamins
    (c) roughage and minerals
    (d) vitamins and minerals

13. A ball is hit on the wall. The direction of the movement of the ball after it hits the wall is changed, this is happened?

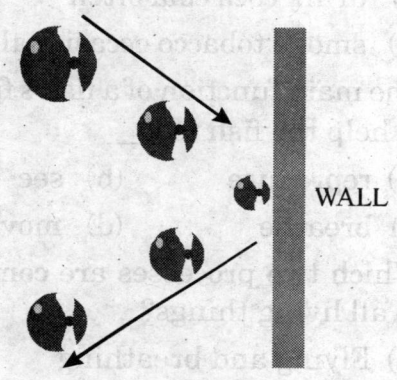

(a) Due to application of force
(b) Due to hardness of the wall
(c) Due to softness of the ball
(d) All of these

14. We sprinkle powder on the carrom board. Why?
(a) To increase friction
(b) To get pleasant smell
(c) To decrease friction
(d) To make the board white so that it looks beautiful

15. The time it takes the Earth to orbit the Sun is one
(a) year
(b) season
(c) month
(d) day

16. A force that pulls two objects together is
(a) speed
(b) friction
(c) force of attraction
(d) inertia

17. In the game of billiards, which type of energy players give to cue the ball by striking it with the cue stick?
(a) Friction
(b) Kinetic energy
(c) mechanical energy
(d) Potential energy

18. The tiny part of a seed that can grow into a plant is the
(a) pistil
(b) spore
(c) fruit
(d) embryo

———————— Space for Rough Work ————————

19. A definite shape and a definite volume are properties of which state of matter?
    (a) Solid only
    (b) Liquid only
    (c) Solid and liquid
    (d) Liquid and gas

20. When a cup of water at room temperature is put in a freezer, the state of water will change from
    (a) liquid to gas
    (b) gas to liquid
    (c) liquid to solid
    (d) solid to liquid

21. During which process are pieces of rock materials being moved over Earth's surface by water and wind?
    (a) Conduction
    (b) Deposition
    (c) Erosion
    (d) Revolution

22. In order to maintain good health, humans should ____.
    (a) eat foods high in fat
    (b) exercise regularly
    (c) drink coca cola often
    (d) smoke tobacco occasionally

23. The main function of a fish's fins is to help the fish to____
    (a) reproduce   (b) see
    (c) breathe   (d) move

24. Which two processes are common to all living things?
    (a) Flying and breathing
    (b) Migrating and reproducing
    (c) Using nutrients and growing
    (d) Eliminating waste and hibernating

25. Trees start as seeds and grow into mature trees that produce more seeds. This pattern represents a _____.
    (a) food chain
    (b) life cycle
    (c) food supply
    (d) life span

───────── Space for Rough Work ─────────

26. What do we call a group of camels together?
    (a) Herd
    (b) Flock
    (c) Gang
    (d) Group

27. Which of the following animals have external ears?
    (a) Snakes
    (b) Lizards
    (c) Insects
    (d) Cows

28. What do we call the roots that are present above the ground?
    (a) Terrestrial roots
    (b) Tap roots
    (c) Aerial roots
    (d) Fibrous Roots

29. Of all the flowers grown in different seasons, not all are edible. Which of the following flowers in the option is not edible?
    (a) Lavender
    (b) Ivy
    (c) Rose
    (d) Jasmine

30. Animals that live in water are known as _____.
    (a) terrestrial animals
    (b) amphibians
    (c) aquatic animals
    (d) aerial animals

31. _____ occurs when pollutants are discharged directly or indirectly into water bodies.
    (a) Water pollution
    (b) Air pollution
    (c) River contamination
    (d) Water spiollage

———————— Space for Rough Work ————————

32. Each of the following containers contain an equal volume of water. In which container will the water evaporate at the slowest rate?

(a) Test tube with water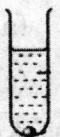

(b) Cup with water

(c) Glass with water

(d) Flat pan with water

33. The method that is used to retain the quality of soil and its mineral content is
(a) crop rotation
(b) terrace farming
(c) afforestation
(d) deforestation

34. When a gas changes into a liquid, it is called _____.
(a) condensation
(b) melting
(c) solidification
(d) evaporation

35. The largest river of India is
(a) Yamuna   (b) Satluj
(c) Ganga   (d) Ravi

―――――― Space for Rough Work ――――――

GENERAL KNOWLEDGE MOCK TEST 1-5

OLYMPIAD Mock Test 1

Name : _____ Max. Marks : 25
Number of Questions : 25 Time : 1 Hour

There is no negative marking in the test.

1. Voice box is a part of the respiratory tract which produces sound. It is also called_____.
   (a) trachea   (b) larynx
   (c) pharynx   (d) oesophagus

2. Select the incorrect match from the following pairs.
   (a) Deer – Herbivore
   (b) Tiger – Carnivore
   (c) Man – Omnivore
   (d) Cow – Carnivore

3. Who is the current President of Russia?
   (a) Donald Trump
   (b) Vladimir Putin
   (c) Emmanual Macron
   (d) Justin Trudean

4. Plant leaves bear small openings through which water vapour and gases are exchanged with the outer environment. What are these openings are called?
   (a) Stomata   (b) Spiracles
   (c) Cuticle   (d) Vein

5. Bakers usually add a substance to flour while making bread. Which of the following is added to the flour?

   (a) Bacteria   (b) Fungi
   (c) Protozoa   (d) Viruses

―――――― Space for Rough Work ――――――

6. A gas is one of the main causes of global warming and is also utilized by plants for performing photosynthesis. Identify the gas.
   (a) Oxygen (b) Nitrogen
   (c) Ozone   (d) Carbon dioxide

7. To which Class of animals do humans belong?
   (a) Reptiles (b) Amphibians
   (c) Birds   (d) Mammals

8. Which of the following Mughal emperors started his own religion Din-e-Ilahi?
   (a) Babur   (b) Aurangzeb
   (c) Akbar   (d) Shahjahan

9. 'Jana Gana Mana' is the national anthem of India. It is the Hindi version of a song originally composed in Bengali by_____.
   (a) Rabindranath Tagore
   (b) Raja Ram Mohan Roy
   (c) Bankim Chandra Chatterjee
   (d) Sri Aurobindo

10. How many spokes are there in 'Ashoka Chakra' situated in our national flag?
    (a) 24   (b) 26
    (c) 25   (d) 22

11. The telescope is one of the most important inventions which helped scientists to observe the Earth and other planets in the universe. Who invented the telescope?

    (a) Isaac Newton
    (b) Hans Christian Anderson
    (c) Hans Lippershey
    (d) Galileo Galilei

Space for Rough Work

12. Read the following statements.

    I. Saturn has beautiful rings surrounding it.

    II. Earth has one large natural satellite, known as the Sun.

    Choose the correct option.

    (a) I is true
    (b) II is true
    (c) Both I and II are true
    (d) Both I and II are false

13. Water cycle is a natural process in nature which helps in maintaining level of water on the Earth and in the environment. Which of the following sequence of events correctly show a water cycle?

    (a) Water released in the atmosphere through evaporation and by plants ⟶ Formation of Cloud ⟶ Condensation ⟶ Rainfall

    (b) Water released in the atmosphere through evaporation and by plants ⟶ Condensation ⟶ Formation of Cloud ⟶ Rainfall

    (c) Condensation ⟶ Water released in the atmosphere through evaporation and by plants ⟶ Formation of Cloud ⟶ Rainfall

    (d) None of these

14. Taj Mahal is known for its beauty but due to some environmental problem it faces degradation. Which of the following might have caused its degradation?

    (a) Acid rain   (b) Lightning
    (c) Storm   (d) Sunlight

15. Niagara Falls was discovered by-

    (a) Alexander Eiffel
    (b) Louis Hennepin
    (c) James Cook
    (d) Jean Henry Durant

─────────── Space for Rough Work ───────────

16. After completing Master's degree, one goes in for higher studies. What does the higher degree PhD stand for?
    (a) Doctor of Philosophy
    (b) Doctor of Politics
    (c) Degree in Philosophy
    (d) None of the above

17. 'The Jungle Book' is a collection of stories by English author Rudyard Kipling. A principal character is the boy Mowgli, who is raised in the jungle by wolves. A powerful snake is one of Mowgli's mentors and friends. What is the name of the snake?

    (a) Baloo   (b) Kaa
    (c) Bagheera (d) Akela

18. This dance form is one of the major forms of classical Indian dance. It involves colourful make-up, costumes and facemasks that the traditionally male actor-dancer wears. It was developed in the Malayalam-speaking southwestern region of India (Kerala).

    Which dance form is being talked about in the above paragraph?
    (a) Bharatanatyam
    (b) Kathakali
    (c) Kuchipudi
    (d) Odissi

19. Which of the following adventure activities is correctly matched to its pictured?

    (a) Caving

    (b) Rafting

    (c) Paragliding

    (d) Trekking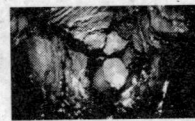

Space for Rough Work

20. With which game is the given player associated?

(a) Cricket (b) Football
(c) Hockey (d) Chess

21. Every game in Olympics has its own pictogram. Which sport does the given pictogram depict?

(a) Football (b) Hockey
(c) Wrestling (d) Archery

22. What does the given traffic sign depict?

(a) No playing on the street
(b) No pedestrian allowed
(c) No passing allowed
(d) No parking allowed

23. Who is the present president of India?
(a) Ram Nath Kovind
(b) Pranab Mukherjee
(c) Pratibha Patil
(d) Draupadi Murmu

24. Which one of the following is the largest coffee growing country in the world?
(a) Brazil (b) Korea
(c) Singapore (d) Belgium

25. The architect of the North and South Blocks of the Central Secretariat in Delhi was-
(a) Herbert Bakers
(b) Sir Edward Lutyens
(c) Robert Tor Russell
(d) Antonin Raymond

Space for Rough Work

OLYMPIAD Mock Test 2

Name: _____
Number of Questions : 25

Max. Marks : 25
Time : 1 Hour

There is no negative marking in the test.

1. Heart plays an important role in circulating blood throughout our body. The heart has four chambers which contain blood for circulation. What is the lower chamber called?

   (a) Auricle　　(b) Ventricle
   (c) Alveoli　　(d) Artery

2. Select the incorrect match from the following pairs.

   (a) Lung --- Alveoli
   (b) Heart --- Auricle
   (c) Kidney --- Neuron
   (d) Eye --- Retina

3. Tear is an important liquid that keeps our eyes in moist condition and prevents eye infection by killing germs. Which of the following glands is responsible for producing tear?

   (a) Lacrimal gland
   (b) Salivary gland
   (c) Pancreas
   (d) Pituitary gland

―――――― *Space for Rough Work* ――――――

4. Which of the following is an example of a plant?
   (a) Bacteria   (b) Yeast
   (c) Petunia   (d) Lichen

5. Which of the following plants is different from other plants?
   (a) Apple   (b) Rose
   (c) Mustard   (d) Cactus

6. Which of the following organisms act as decomposers and help in recycling of matter in the environment?

   (a) Bacteria

   (b) Virus

   (c) Fungi

   (d) Both (a) and (c)

7. When an animal takes the appearance of its environment for protection, it is called_____.
   (a) hibernation   (b) aestivation
   (c) camouflage   (d) migration

8. What is the currency of Switzerland?
   (a) Krone   (b) Franc
   (c) Dollar   (d) Ringgit

9. Lord Buddha was born in
   (a) Lumbini   (b) Vaishali
   (c) Bodh Gaya   (d) Patliputra

10. Identify the country whose national flag is given below.

    (a) Bhutan   (b) Burma
    (c) Sri Lanka   (d) Nepal

Space for Rough Work

11. He was a Greek mathematician and astronomer who became the chief librarian at the Library of Alexandria. He invented the discipline of geography and is known for calculating the circumference of the Earth. Who is being talked about in the above paragraph?

(a) Aryabhatta (b) Galileo
(c) Archimedes (d) Eratosthenes

12. The device dynamo is used to convert
    (a) electrical energy into heat energy.
    (b) electrical energy into light energy.
    (c) mechanical energy into electrical energy.
    (d) heat energy into light energy.

13. The liquid that comes out of a volcano is called_____.
    (a) magma
    (b) lava
    (c) water
    (d) oil

14. What is the name of Edison's motion picture invention?
    (a) Film
    (b) Kinetoscope
    (c) Phonoscope
    (d) Moviescope

15. Which of the following indicates sulphur dioxide more pollution?
    (a) Mosses
    (b) Lichens
    (c) Algal Blooms
    (d) None of these

16. Study the given diagram. What can the car owner do to reduce the air pollution caused by his car?

    (a) Use a bigger exhaust pipe.
    (b) Seal the exhaust pipe with a plastic bag.
    (c) Check the quality of tyres.
    (d) Send the car for regular servicing.

17. Which of the following statements is/are true?
    (a) Cutting down of trees is called reforestation.
    (b) Tree cutting causes more rainfall.
    (c) CNG is less polluting than diesel.
    (d) Terrace farming does not help in preventing landslides.

18. Greta Thunberg, a teenage environment activist, hails from--
    (a) Sweden   (b) Germany
    (c) The USA   (d) Canada

19. Which of the following awards was instituted by Shanti Prasad Jain?
    (a) Vyas Samman
    (b) Shankar Samman
    (c) Jnanpith Award
    (d) Kabir Award

20. When was the first Olympic Games held?
    (a) 1896   (b) 1898
    (c) 1873   (d) 1891

21. Which of the following cricketers has scored most runs in one-day international cricket?
    (a) Sachin Tendulkar
    (b) Ricky Ponting
    (c) Sanath Jayasuriya
    (d) Rahul Dravid

─────────── Space for Rough Work ───────────

22. The Kyaik Htee Yoe pagoda is located in _____
    (a) Nepal (b) Myanmar
    (c) Bhutan (d) Sri Lanka

23. In which country did External Affairs Minister Dr S Jaishankar inaugurate the bridge built by India?
    (a) Ghana (b) Senegal
    (c) Mozambique (d) Sri Lanka

24. According to the Tiger Census, how much population of tigers in India increase by the year 2022?
    (a) 3167 (b) 3100
    (c) 3267 (d) 3334

25. Who has become the fastest batsman to score 6000 runs in IPL history?
    (a) Virat Kohli
    (b) David Warner
    (c) Rohit Sharma
    (d) K L Rahul

OLYMPIAD Mock Test 3

Name : _____
Number of Questions : 25

Max. Marks : 25
Time : 1 Hour

There is no negative marking in the test.

1. Which type of tooth is pointed, sharp, and helps to tear food?

   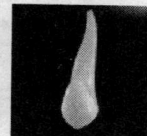

   (a) Molars (b) Premolars
   (c) Incisors (d) Canines

2. Select the incorrect match from the following pairs.
   (a) Urine formation--Kidney
   (b) Blood circulation-- Heart
   (c) Blood oxygenation--Liver
   (d) Food digestion--Stomach

3. Egg is rich in_____.
   (a) starch (b) glucose
   (c) protein (d) carbohydrates

4. Which of the following is the smallest bone in our body?
   (a) Tibia (b) Carpel
   (c) Humerus (d) Stapes

5. Which of the following is not required by plants to prepare food?
   (a) Water
   (b) Carbon dioxide
   (c) Light
   (d) Oxygen

— Space for Rough Work —

6. Cockroaches breathe through____.
   (a) spiracles (b) skin
   (c) lungs (d) gills

7. The natural home of an animal is called_____.
   (a) house (b) water
   (c) nest (d) habitat

8. Which of the following is an example of stem modification?
   (a) Ginger (b) Radish
   (c) Carrot (d) Beetroot

9. What are the people of Tibet called?
   (a) Tibetans (b) Tibs
   (c) Tibetanins (d) Tibets

10. The bird in the given figure is the national bird of_____.
    (a) Australia (b) New Zealand
    (c) Nepal (d) Finland

11. This is the closest star system to the Solar System. It consists of three stars. Identify the star system.
    (a) Alnitak (b) Alpha Centauri
    (c) Aldebaran (d) Antares

12. Which of the following can be attracted by magnets?
    (a) Iron (b) Plastic
    (c) Paper (d) Wood

13. Which of the following statements is/are true?
    (a) Fertilizers cause water pollution.
    (b) Carbon dioxide causes global warming.
    (c) Both of these are true
    (d) None of these are true

14. Match the following and choose the correct option.

   Column I   **Column II**
   (a) Soil Pollution   1. Lung disease
   (b) Water pollution   2. Minamata
   (c) Air pollution   3. Barren Land
                          4. Acid Rain

   (a) a-1, b-2, c-3 (b) a-1, b-4, c-3
   (c) a-3, b-2, c-1 (d) a-1, b-2, c-4

15. Which of the following practices improve soil fertility without damaging the environment?
   (a) Use of chemical fertilizer
   (b) Crop rotation
   (c) Use of bio-fertilizer
   (d) Both (b) and (c)

16. India is participating in the SLINEX-2023 Maritime Exercise with which country?
   (a) Singapore   (b) Sri Lanka
   (c) Seychelles (d) Bhutan

17. Who among the following authors is also known as the 'Shakespeare of India'?
   (a) Kalidas
   (b) Premchand
   (c) Rabindranath Tagore
   (d) None of the above

18. Which country has become the 31st member of NATO?
   (a) Finland   (b) Sweden
   (c) Japan   (d) Brazil

19. He is the classical Indian musician known for playing Sarod. He has received the prestigious award Padma Vibhushan in 2001.

   Who is being talked about in the above paragraph?

   (a) Ali Akbar Khan
   (b) Amjad Ali Khan

(c) Ravi Shankar
(d) Shiv Kumar Sharma

20. Which of the following is the national sport of Italy?
    (a) Hockey   (b) Football
    (c) Basketball (d) Tennis

21. Who has been appointed as the new Executive Director of the Reserve Bank of India?
    (a) Neeraj Nigam
    (b) Ajay Maken
    (c) Ashok Sinha
    (d) Amit Anand

22. Which African country is going to launch its first operational Earth observation satellite?
    (a) Kenya   (b) Namibia
    (c) Morocco (d) Zimbabwe

23. Who has become the highest wicket-taker in the T20I format of cricket?
    (a) Shakib Al Hasan
    (b) Ravindra Jadeja
    (c) Adam Zampa
    (d) Kuldeep Yadav

24. Which of the following cities has India's first multi-sports museum?

    (a) Kolkata   (b) Bangaluru
    (c) Hyderabad (d) Delhi

25. Who has been honoured with the Highest Civilian Award of Assam for the year 2023 'Assam Baibhav'?
    (a) Yogi Adityanath
    (b) Anuj Mehta
    (c) Piyush Goyal
    (d) Dr. Tapan Saikia

─────── *Space for Rough Work* ───────

OLYMPIAD
Mock Test 4

Name: _____
Number of Questions : 40

Max. Marks : 40
Time : 2 Hours

There is no negative marking in the test.

1. Which of the following organs is not used during digestion?
   (a) Stomach   (b) Small intestine
   (c) Liver   (d) Lung

2. Select the incorrect match from the following pairs.
   (a) Protein--Egg
   (b) Carbohydrate--Rice
   (c) Fibre__Meat
   (d) Fat—Ghee

3. There would be no urine formation in the body if which of the following organs is removed?
   (a) Heart   (b) Kidney
   (c) Liver   (d) Lung

4. The fluids in the human eye are called
   (a) Aqueous humour
   (b) Vitreous humour
   (c) Amniotic fluid and pleural fluid
   (d) Both (a) and (b)

5. Functions of plant roots include
   (a) Absorbtion of water from soil
   (b) Absorbtion of nutrients from soil
   (c) Anchoring plant in the soil
   (d) All of the above

―――――――― Space for Rough Work ――――――――

6. Some animals undergo a state of inactivity during winter. It is known as
   (a) Aestivation (b) Hibernation
   (c) Adaptation (d) Acclimatization

7. Match the columns given below.

   Column I   **Column II**
   a. Stomata   1. Human being
   b. Lungs   2. Earthworm
   c. Gills   3. Plants
   d. Skin   4. Fish

   (a) a-1, b-2, c-3, d-4
   (b) a-3, b-1, c-4, d-2
   (c) a-1, b-4, c-3, d-2
   (d) a-4, b-2, c-3, d-1

8. Which part of the venus flytrap plant is modified into a structure that is used to trap insects?

   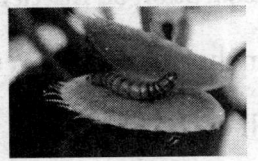

   (a) Stem   (b) Leaf
   (c) Root   (d) Flower

9. This Indian classical dance is one of the two classical dances of India that developed and remains popular in the state of Kerala. The dance form dance gets its name from the word Mohini – a mythical enchantress avatar of the Hindu god Vishnu. Which dance form is being talked about?

   (a) Kathakali
   (b) Kuchipudi
   (c) Mohiniyattam
   (d) Bharatnatyam

10. The ancient art of India can be seen in the murals in the caves of Maharashtra. Besides murals, there are magnificent stone

Space for Rough Work

sculptures of Hindu deities, the Buddha and Jain Thirthankaras. There are three such caves which have been declared UNESCO World Heritage Sites. Two caves are the Ajanta and the Elephanta. Which is the third one?

(a) Aihole caves
(b) Badami caves
(c) Ellora caves
(d) Caves at Aurangabad

11. She is an American astronaut and United States Navy officer of Indian-Slovenian race. She formerly held the records for most number of spacewalks by a woman and most spacewalk time for a woman (50 hours, 40 minutes). She was assigned to the International Space Station as a member of Expedition 14 and Expedition 15. Who is being talked about?

(a) Valentina Tereshkova
(b) Kalpana Chawla
(c) Sunita Williams
(d) Laika

12. The discovery of the laws of floating bodies was considered an important achievement for the movement of boats and ships on the surface of water. Who is credited with this discovery?

(a) Isaac Newton
(b) Galileo
(c) Archimedes
(d) Joseph J. Thomson

13. Which of the following is/are non-biodegradable?

(a) Paper (b) Plastic toys
(c) Credit card (d) Both (b) and (c)

——————— *Space for Rough Work* ———————

14. Which of these is a type of green energy?
    (a) A petrol pump
    (b) A coal burning fire
    (c) A wind turbine
    (d) An electric cable

15. Given below are a few steps to prepare brownies along with their codes.
    1. We stirred the ingredients together.
    2. The brownies cooked in the oven for 15 minutes.
    3. We ate the brownies.
    Choose the option which shows correct sequence of steps.
    (a) 2, 1, 3   (b) 3, 2, 1
    (c) 1, 2, 3   (d) 1, 3, 2

16. Who has been enrolled in the Bar Council of the state as the first transgender lawyer in Kerala?
    (a) Vidya Kamble
    (b) Padma Lakshmi
    (c) Swati Bidhan Barua
    (d) Joyita Mandal

17. According to the World Happiness Report 2023, which country is the happiest country in the world?
    (a) Denmark   (b) Iceland
    (c) Israel   (d) Finland

18. 'Shinku La Pass', which was seen in the news, is located in which state?
    (a) Uttarakhand
    (b) Arunachal Pradesh
    (c) Himachal Pradesh
    (d) Sikkim

19. 'Charlotte's Web' is a children's novel by American author E. B. White. The novel tells the story of a pig named Wilbur and his

friendship with a barn spider. When Wilbur is in danger of being slaughtered by the farmer, the spider writes messages praising Wilbur in her web in order to persuade the farmer to let him live. What is the name of the spider?

(a) Charlotte (b) Templeton
(c) Arable   (d) Fussy

20. The Chamera Dam is located in which state/UT?
 (a) Puducherry
 (b) Uttar Pradesh
 (c) Himachal Pradesh
 (d) Jharkhand

21. Uttar Pradesh shares it borders with how many states?
 (a) 5   (b) 6
 (c) 7   (d) 8

22. Who played the role of Milkha Singh in the film "Bhaag Milkha Bhaag"?
 (a) Salman Khan
 (b) Aamir Khan
 (c) Saif Ali Khan
 (d) Farhan Akhtar

23. 'Godan' is a Hindi novel, which has been translated into English as 'The Gift of a Cow'. It was first published in 1936 and is considered one of the greatest Hindustani novels of modern Indian literature. Who has written the novel?
 (a) Rabindranath Tagore
 (b) Munshi Premchand
 (c) Kalidas
 (d) Yashpal

———————— *Space for Rough Work* ————————

24. Down Syndrome is also known as:
    (a) Edwards syndrome
    (b) Patau syndrome
    (c) Mongolism
    (d) None of the above

25. 'Shivkumar Sharma' who passed away recently, is known for popularising which musical instrument?
    (a) Bansuri   (b) Santoor
    (c) Sitar   (d) Sarangi

26. 'Baba Saheb Ambedkar Yatra Tour' is a part of which initiative?
    (a) Dekho Apna Desh
    (b) PRASAD
    (c) PARAKH
    (d) VIKAS

27. Which game is shown in the picture given below?

    (a) Polo   (b) Rugby
    (c) Billiards   (d) Triathlon

28. Aligators and crocodiles belong to the class of _____.
    (a) fish   (b) amphilians
    (c) reptiles   (d) mammals

29. India's first pure green hydrogen plant has been commissioned in which state?
    (a) Gujarat   (b) Assam
    (c) West Bengal (d) Odisha

30. First living organism to spend seven days in space was a dog. It was sent in the space craft named sputik 2. what was the name of the dog?
    (a) Ham   (b) Laika
    (c) Snoopy   (d) Benji

31. Our body contains several chemical substances which help in the digestion of food. These substances are called
    (a) Hormones   (b) Catalysts
    (c) Enzymes   (d) Starchs

32. Which of the following is true?
    (a) Skin is not an organ.
    (b) Alcohol consumption damages the liver.

(c) Humans can control heart beat.

(d) Plants do not require carbon dioxide.

33. Tomato plant is a _____.

(a) herb (b) shrubs
(c) tree (d) climber

34. Which part of the camel is used to store fat?

(a) Neck
(b) Stomach
(c) Hump
(d) Mouth

35. Which of the following diseases is caused by bacteria?

(a) Typhoid
(b) Influenza
(c) Ringworm
(d) Malaria

36. Which of the following vitamins is found in lemon?

(a) Vitamin A   (b) Vitamin C
(c) Vitamin K   (d) Vitamin D

37. Which of the following processes can be used to prevent food from getting spoiled?

(a) Heating
(b) Cooling
(c) Drying
(d) All the above

38. Which of the following organisms uses sound to locate food?

(a)

(b)

(c)

(d)

Space for Rough Work

39. Chameleon in a type of lizard that can change its colour to escape from its enemies. This process in called_____.
    (a) camouflage
    (b) moulting
    (c) hibernation
    (d) migration

40. Which of the following can cause death in a closed room?
    (a) Carbon dioxide
    (b) Ozone
    (c) Carbon monoxide
    (d) Methane

OLYMPIAD Mock Test 5

Name: _____
Number of Questions : 40

Max. Marks : 40
Time : 2 Hours

There is no negative marking in the test.

1. Windpipe is a tube that allows the passage of air in almost all air-breathing animals with lungs. The windpipe is also called as
   (a) Trachea (b) Larynx
   (c) Pharynx (d) Diaphragm

2. Which of the following can be eaten raw, after washing?
   (a) Radish (b) Potato
   (c) Brinjal (d) Bitter gourd

3. Which of the following does not have any function in the body?
   (a) Bile duct   (b) Urethra
   (c) Gall Bladder (d) Appendix

4. Which of the following organs is damaged by alcohol consumption?
   (a) Lungs (b) Stomach
   (c) Skin   (d) Liver

5. How many bones do adult human beings have?
   (a) 209 (b) 206
   (c) 190 (d) 220

6. Which of the following pigments is responsible for providing colour to human skin?
   (a) Melanin
   (b) Carotene
   (c) Chlorophyll
   (d) Haemoglobin

———————————— Space for Rough Work ————————————

7. Yeast is a kind of
   (a) fungi   (b) virus
   (c) bacteria (d) plant

8. Which of the following happens only in plants, not in animals?
   (a) Respiration
   (b) Reproduction
   (c) Photosynthesis
   (d) Growth

9. The colourful parts of flowers that protect the flower parts where seeds are made are called_____.

   (a) petals   (b) stamens
   (c) pistils (d) sepals

10. Monkeys belong to the category of _____.

    (a) terrestrial animals
    (b) aerial animals
    (c) arboreal animals
    (d) aquatic animals

11. Building blocks of the body are
    (a) glucose (b) fats
    (c) proteins (d) vitamins

12. Which of the following juices is secreted by liver?

    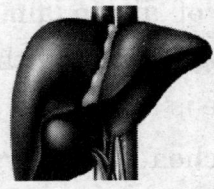

    (a) Saliva (b) Pepsin
    (d) Bile   (d) Trypsin

13. Which of the following help bears to live in cold condition in winter months?

(a) Hunting
(b) Fishing
(c) Hibernation
(d) Aestivation

14. In India, which state is called Orchid Paradise?
    (a) Arunachal Pradesh
    (b) Himachal Pradesh
    (c) Jammu & Kashmir
    (d) Uttarakhand

15. Column I shows the name of states and column II depicts their chief ministers.

Column I	Column II
a. Goa	1. Manohar Parrikar
b. Odisha	2. Sarbananda Sonowal
c. Sikkim	3. Naveen Patnaik
d. Assam	4. Pawan Kumar Chamling

    Choose the correct option.
    (a) a-1, b-2, c-3, d-4
    (b) a-4, b-1, c-3, d-2
    (c) a-1, b-3, c-4, d-2
    (d) a-4, b-3, c-2, d-1

16. Which of the following is the largest museum in India?

    (a) Indian Museum, Kolkata
    (b) National Museum of India, Delhi
    (c) Salar Jung Museum, Hyderabad
    (d) Gandhi Smriti, Delhi

17. Which of the following spacecrafts is sent to Saturn planet?

    (a) Messenger   (b) Curiosity
    (c) Cassini   (d) Skylab

Space for Rough Work

18. She was the first American of Indian origin to explore space. She first flew on Space Shuttle Columbia in 1997 as a mission specialist. In 2003, she was one of the seven crew members who died in the Space Shuttle Columbia disaster. Who among the following is being described here?

   (a)    (b)

   (c)    (d)

19. Which of the following travels with maximum speed?
    (a) Airplane (b) Light
    (c) Bullet Train (d) Meteors

20. Which instrument is used to detect/record earthquakes?
    (a) Richter scale
    (b) Seismograph
    (c) Thermometer
    (d) Barometer

21. Read the following statements.
    1. I am present in the air.
    2. No organism can live without me.
    3. I am produced by plants.
    These statements are regarding
    (a) carbon dioxide
    (b) oxygen
    (c) nitrogen
    (d) hydrogen

22. Read the following statements.
    A. Soil erosion may be increased by cutting down trees in a forest.
    B. Coal is renewable resource.
    Choose the correct option.
    (a) A is true
    (b) B is true
    (c) Both A and B are true
    (d) Both A and B are false

───────────── *Space for Rough Work* ─────────────

23. Which of the following activities can help in preventing soil erosion?
    (a) Terrace farming
    (b) Tree plantation
    (c) Grazing
    (d) Both (a) and (b)

24. Which of the following causes pollution?
    (a) Oil spill in the ocean
    (b) Burning fossil fuels
    (c) Littering trash on the ground
    (d) All of the above

25. Chhello Show, which was announced India's official entry to the Oscars 2023, is a film made in which language?
    (a) Kannada   (b) Gujarati
    (c) Marathi   (d) Hindi

26. Gurram Jashuva, who was also known as 'People's Poet' is from which state?
    (a) Kerala
    (b) Andhra Pradesh
    (c) Assam
    (d) Odisha

27. 'Nankana Sahib' is a Sikh pilgrimage place located in which country?
    (a) India   (b) Pakistan
    (c) Nepal   (d) Bangladesh

28. 'Titanic' is a 1997 American Hollywood film, which is based on the sinking of the ship 'RMS Titanic', and features stars like Leonardo DiCaprio and Kate Winslet. Who directed the film?

———————— *Space for Rough Work* ————————

(a) David Fincher
(b) James Cameron
(c) Clint Eastwood
(d) Michael Bay

29. Kangra miniature painting, which was seen in the news, is made in which state?

    (a) Gujarat
    (b) Himachal Pradesh
    (c) Assam
    (d) Arunachal Pradesh

30. 'Hornbill Festival' is the flagship cultural event of which Indian state?

    (a) Assam
    (b) Nagaland
    (c) Sikkim
    (d) Arunachal Pradesh

31. "Bodhisiri" is a cruise boat operated by which state tourism department?

    (a) Kerala
    (b) Karnataka
    (c) Andhra Pradesh
    (d) Tamil Nadu

32. Which of the following is not an aerobic exercise?

    (a) Walking
    (b) Jumping
    (c) Talking
    (d) Swimming

33. Which state has announced plans to install automatic sirens to protect elephants from accidents?

    (a) Kerala
    (b) Madhya Pradesh
    (c) Maharashtra
    (d) Odisha

――――――― Space for Rough Work ―――――――

34. When should your family make a fire escape plan?

   (a) Never. My family does not need a plan.
   (b) After you have called to report the fire.
   (c) Before there is a fire in your home.
   (d) When the smoke alarm beeps.

35. What should you do if you need to cross the street?

   (a) Ask an adult to help if you are under age 10.
   (b) Look left, right and left again for traffic.
   (c) Make sure drivers see you.
   (d) All of the above

36. When is world environment Day celebrated?

   (a) 7th July   (b) 5th June
   (c) 30th June   (d) 5th October

37. Name the microwave sterilizer which was developed by Pune-based Defence Institute of Advanced Technology (DIAT), to disintegrate coronavirus by heating.

   (a) Sara   (b) Sindhya
   (c) Jackqueen   (d) Atulya

38. Bile is collected in _____?

   (a) Liver
   (b) Gall Bladder
   (c) Duodenum Canal
   (d) Spleen

39. With which of the following diseases Project Kavach is related to?
    (a) Malaria   (b) Dengue
    (c) AIDS   (d) Swineflu

40. Who is the current Chief Minister of Delhi?
    (a) Narendra Modi
    (b) Arvind Kejriwal
    (c) Sushma Swaraj
    (d) Sonia Gandhi

LOGICAL REASONING MOCK TEST 1-5

OLYMPIAD Mock Test 1

Name : _____
Number of Questions : 30
Max. Marks : 30
Time : 1 Hour 30 Minutes

There is no negative marking in the test.

1. What are the next two numbers in the pattern below?

    8, 10, 14, 20, __?__ , __?__

    (a) 28, 30 (b) 30, 28
    (c) 28, 38 (d) 20, 30

DIRECTION : In the question, some letters are given which are numbered 1, 2, 3, 4, 5 and 6 followed by four options containing combinations of these numbers. Find the combination of numbers so that letters arranged accordingly form a meaningful word.

2. I P E L O C
   1 2 3 4 5 6

    (a) 3, 4, 5, 1, 2, 6
    (b) 4, 5, 1, 2, 3, 6
    (c) 2, 5, 4, 1, 6, 3
    (d) 1, 4, 3, 5, 2, 6

DIRECTIONS : Find out the word which CANNOT be made from the letters of the given words.

3. REASONABLE
    (a) BRAIN   (b) BONES
    (c) NOBLE   (d) ARSON

4. If 'Green' is called 'Red', 'Red' is called 'Yellow' and 'Yellow' is called 'Blue', what is the colour of parrot?
    (a) Green   (b) Red
    (c) Yellow   (d) Blue

5. In a certain code ROPE is written as $3%6 and RITE is written as $4#6. How is PORT written in that code?
    (a) %4$#   (b) $3%#
    (c) $64%   (d) %3$#

Space for Rough Work

DIRECTIONS (Qs. 6 to 8) : Look at the figure below and answer the following questions.

6. Which tree is 3rd to the left of second tree from right end?

   (a) Q   (b) T
   (c) R   (d) S

7. If tree Q and S interchange their positions, then which of the following trees is adjacent to Q?

   (a) P   (b) Q
   (c) R   (d) U

8. If tree R is removed from the row, then which tree is in middle of the row?

   (a) P   (b) Q
   (c) S   (d) T

DIRECTIONS : Which of the following figures is the mirror image of figure (X)?

9.

   (a) 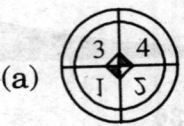   (b)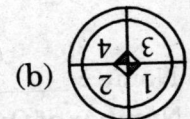

   (c)    (d)

DIRECTION : Find the mirror image of combination of letters.

10. BHSIP

    (a) ꟼISHB
    (b) PISHB
    (c) PISHB
    (d) ꟼISHB

DIRECTIONS (Qs. 11 & 12) : One problem figure is followed by four options. In one of the options, the figure similar to the problem figure is exactly embedded/hidden without any orientation. Find the option.

─── Space for Rough Work ───

Mock Test-1

11.

(a)    (b)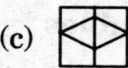

(c) 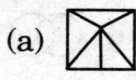   (d)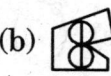

12.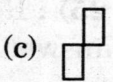

(a) 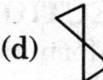   (b) (image)

(c) (image)   (d) (image)

DIRECTION (Q. 13) : Use the figure given below to answer the questions.

13. If P and Q interchange their positions and S and R interchange their positions, then S and Q move diagonally and meet at the centre. P is in _____ of S.

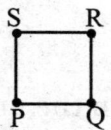

(a) South-east
(b) South-west
(c) North-east
(d) North-west

14. Garima walks towards east, after travelling some distance she takes a left turn and again travels some distance. She again turns to left. In which direction she will be facing now?

(a) North   (b) East
(c) West   (d) South

15. If the day before yesterday was Friday, what day will be day after tomorrow?

(a) Friday   (b) Thursday
(c) Wednesday   (d) Tuesday

16. Rohan's birthday falls on the day just after 4th Monday of the January 20XX. The day on which Rohan celebrates his birthday is _____.

January 20XX						
S	M	T	W	Th	F	S
	1	2	3			

(a) 21st   (b) 23rd
(c) 22nd   (d) 26th

DIRECTION (Q. 17) : There is a certain relationship between the pair of figures on the either side of : :. Identify the relationship and find the missing figure.

17. 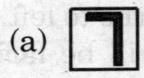 : 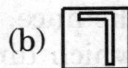 ::  : ?

(a) 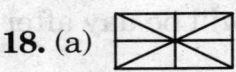 (b) (image)

(c) (image) (d) (image)

DIRECTION (Q. 18) : Find odd one out.

18. (a) (image) (b) (image)

(c) (image) (d) (image)

19. Find the number which when added to itself 13 times, gives 112.
    (a) 6 (b) 10
    (c) 8 (d) 4

20. How many rectangles and circles are there in the given picture?

(a) 8 and 10 (b) 10 and 5
(c) 8 and 12 (d) 8 and 9

21. Which of the following Venn-diagram correctly illustrates the relationship among the classes.

Carrot, Food, Vegetables

(a) (image) (b) (image)

(c) (image) (d) (image)

DIRECTIONS (Qs. 22 to 25) : Read the information carefully to answer the questions.

Anu, Preeti, Rahul, Manu, Kanika and Zara are sitting in a row. Kanika and Zara are in the centre. Anu and Preeti are at the ends. Rahul is sitting to the left of Anu.

22. Who is sitting right to the Rahul?
    (a) Zara (b) Manu
    (c) Anu   (d) Preeti

23. Who sits in the middle of the row?
    (a) Preeti and Anu
    (b) Kanika and Zara

Mock Test-1

(c) Manu and Rahul

(d) Zara and Rahul

24. Which one of the following statements is correct?

   (a) Zara sits third to the right of Anu.
   (b) Kanika is sitting second to the left of Rahul.
   (c) Preeti and Anu are neighbours.
   (d) None of the above

25. Who is sitting immediate left of Kanika?

   (a) Manu   (b) Kanika
   (c) Anu   (d) Preeti

26. Select from four alternative diagrams, the one that best illustrates the relationship among the three classes.

   Pigeons, Birds, Dogs

   (a)    (b)

   (d)    (d)

27. Complete the picture.

   (a) 🦁   (b) 🦄
   (c) 🐵   (d) 🐸

28. In the question, a piece of paper is folded and cut and then folded. One of the four options resembles the unfolded paper. Select the correct option.

   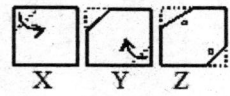
   X   Y   Z

   (a)   (b)
   (c)   (d)

29. Find the water image of the given picture.

———————— *Space for Rough Work* ————————

(a)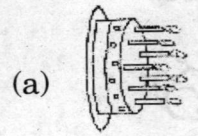

(b)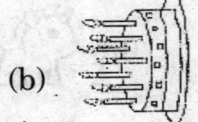

(c)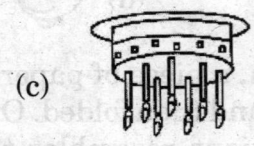

(d)

30. The figure below shows six containers filled with water to the brim. What is the total volume of water in the six containers?

(a) 5000 ml
(b) 4 litres 50 ml
(c) 900 ml
(d) 4500 ml

Space for Rough Work

OLYMPIAD
Mock Test 2

Name : _____
Number of Questions : 30
There is no negative marking in the test.
Max. Marks : 30
Time : 1 Hour 30 Minutes

1. Find the missing number.

   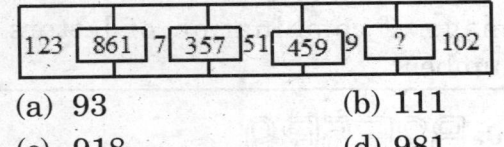

   (a) 93 (b) 111
   (c) 918 (d) 981

DIRECTION : In the question, some letters are given which are numbered 1, 2, 3, 4, 5 and 6 followed by four options containing combinations of these numbers. Find the combination of numbers so that letters arranged accordingly form a meaningful word.

2. T R I F U
   1 2 3 4 5
   (a) 4, 2, 5, 3, 1
   (b) 4, 3, 2, 1, 5
   (c) 5, 3, 2, 1, 4
   (d) 3, 1, 2, 4, 5

DIRECTION (Q. 3) : Find out the word which CANNOT be made from the letters of the given words.

3. CONSCIOUS
   (a) SON (b) COIN
   (c) SUN (d) NOSE

4. In a certain code BOARD is written as 54#12 and MORE is written as 941$. How is DREAM written in that code?
   (a) 21$#9 (b) 21$#9
   (c) 51$#9 (d) 25$#9

5. If 'Frog' is called 'Lizard', 'Lizard' is called 'Fish', 'Fish' is called 'Snake' and 'Snake' is called 'Mole', then to which is fisherman related?

─────── Space for Rough Work ───────

(a) Snake   (b) Lizard
(c) Fish   (d) Frog

DIRECTIONS (6&7): Ten balls are put in a row. Look at the figure and answer the questions based on it.

6. If two more balls are added on the left of ball 1, how many balls will be on right of ball 4?
   (a) 6   (b) 5
   (c) 4   (d) 7

7. If two more balls are added between ball 5 and 6, how many balls, are there between ball 3 and ball 9?
   (a) 5   (b) 6
   (c) 7   (d) 9

8. Nitika ranks eighteenth in a class of 27 students. What is her rank from the last?
   (a) 10   (b) 12
   (c) 14   (d) 16

DIRECTION (Q. 9): Which of the following figures is the mirror image of figure?

(a) MATHS (mirrored vertically)
(b) SHTAM (mirrored)
(c) MATHS (mirrored)
(d) MATHS (mirrored)

DIRECTION (Q. 10): Find the mirror image of combination of letters or numbers.

10. B2E5R9
    (a) 9R5E2B   (b) B2E5R9 (mirrored)
    (c) B2E5R9 (mirrored)   (d) B2E5R9 (mirrored)

DIRECTIONS (11&12): One problem figure is followed by four options. In one of the options, the figure similar to the problem figure is exactly embedded/hidden without any orientation. Find the option.

11. Z

────── Space for Rough Work ──────

(a) 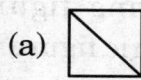 (b)

14. Which point is in north of S?
(a) V (b) T
(c) R (d) U

(c) 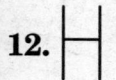 (d)

15. If the second day of a 30 day month is Friday, which of the following would be the last day of the month?
(a) Sunday (b) Monday
(c) Tuesday (d) Friday

12.

(a) 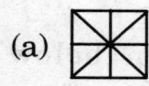 (b)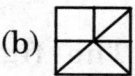

16. Garima's birthday falls on the next day of her parents anniversary. Her parents anniversary will be on 2nd Sunday of July 20XX. When will Garima celebrate her birthday?

(c)  (d)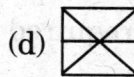

DIRECTIONS (13 & 14) : Use the figure given below to answer the questions.

July 20XX						
S	M	T	W	Th	F	S
		1	2	3		

(a) 13th (b) 14th
(c) 15th (d) 16th

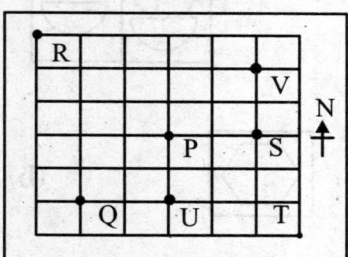

13. Which point is in south-east of P?
(a) T (b) R
(c) Q (d) V

DIRECTION : There is a certain relationship between the pair of figures on the either side of : :. Identify the relationship and find the missing figure.

Space for Rough Work

17.

(a)  (b)

(c)  (d)

DIRECTION (18) : Find odd one out.

18. (a) 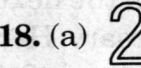 (b)

(c) (d)

19. What is the weight of the teddy bear in the adjoining figure?

(a) 400 g (b) 450 g
(c) 300 g (d) 600 g

20. Which of the following figures below is not a symmetric figure?

(a) 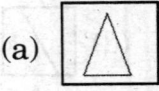 (b)

(c)  (d)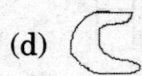

21. The figure X given below is incomplete. Which option figure is required to complete the figure?

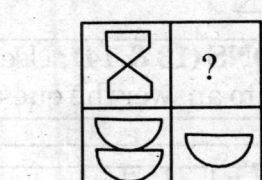

(a) 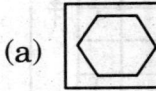 (b)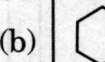

(c)  (d)

22. Select from the five alternative diagrams, the one that best illustrates the relationship among the three classes :

———————— *Space for Rough Work* ————————

Mock Test-2 LR-11

Truck, Ship, Goods

(a)  (b)

(c) 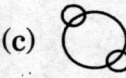 (d)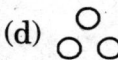

23. In the following question, a square transparent sheet with a pattern is given. Figure out from amongst the four alternatives as to how the pattern would appear when the transparent sheet is folded at the dotted line.

(a) 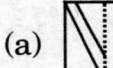 (b)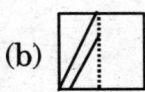

(c) 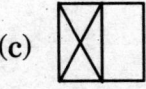 (d)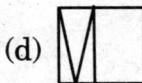

24. How many triangles are there in the given figure?

(a) 5 (b) 7
(c) 9 (d) 10

DIRECTIONS (25 to 29) : Study the information carefully and answer the questions.

Six girls are sitting in a circle. Annie is facing Beenu. Beenu is to the right of Esha and left of Cheenu. Cheenu is to the left of Deepu. Lovely is to the right of Annie. Now, Deepu exchanges her seat with Lovely and Esha with Beenu.

25. Who will be sitting to the left of Deepu?
    (a) Esha   (b) Annie
    (c) Cheenu   (d) Lovely

26. Who will be sitting to the left of Cheenu?
    (a) Annie   (b) Beenu
    (c) Esha   (d) Lovely

27. Who will be sitting opposite to Annie?
    (a) Lovely   (b) Esha
    (c) Beenu   (d) Deepu

——————— *Space for Rough Work* ———————

28. Who are the neighbours of Lovely?
(a) Cheenu, Annie
(b) Esha, Lovely
(c) Deepu, Esha
(d) None of these

29. Which statement is correct regarding Annie?
(a) Annie faces Beenu.
(b) Annie is sitting second to the right of Esha.
(c) Annie is sitting next to Cheenu.
(d) Annie is sitting to the right of lovely.

30. Find the water image of the following picture.

(a)    (b)

(c) 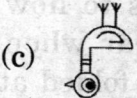   (d)

Space for Rough Work

OLYMPIAD Mock Test 3

Name : _____
Number of Questions : 25
Max. Marks : 25
Time : 1 Hour

There is no negative marking in the test.

1. Identify the rule followed in the number series given below.

   ② ④ ⑧ ⑯ ㉜ ㉞ ⑫⑧

   (a) Add 2 in previous term to get the next term.
   (b) Multiply previous terms by 2 to get the next term.
   (c) Subtract 2, 4 .... sequentially.
   (d) Multiply the number by itself to get the next term.

DIRECTION (Q. 2): Find the category of given word so formed by the combination of letters arranged accordingly to form a meaningful word.

2. R A S T
   (a) Gives light
   (b) Give water
   (c) Gives news
   (d) Gives money

DIRECTION (Q. 3) : Choose one word which can be formed from the letters of the given word.

3. MEASUREMENT
   (a) MASTER
   (b) MANTLE
   (c) SUMMIT
   (d) ASSURE

4. If 'City' is called 'Village', 'Village' is called ' Forest' and 'Forest' is called 'Building', then where do deers live?
   (a) City
   (b) Village
   (c) Forest
   (d) Building

Space for Rough Work

5. If in a certain language LATE is coded as 8&4$ and HIRE is coded as 7*3$, then how will HAIL be coded in the same language?

   (a) 7&8* (b) &7*8
   (c) 7*&8 (d) 7&*8

6. If flowers are arranged in the order from P to W (as in alphabetical series), then how many flowers are to the left of U?

   (a) 5 (b) 6
   (c) 3 (d) 4

7. If the numbers given below are arranged in ascending order, then which number will be in the middle place?

   110, 315, 913, 517, 593, 890, 193, 498, 423, 723, 973

   (a) 498 (b) 517
   (c) 423 (d) 593

8. In a race competition, there are 5 finalists.

   Sapna : She stood just after Megha.

   Riya : She has only one girl behind her.

   Megha : She is not the first.

   Kirti : She is after Sapna.

   Komal : She is before Riya.

   _____ and _____ stood at first and last positions respectively.

   (a) Kirti, Sapna
   (b) Sapna, Riya
   (c) Komal, Kirti
   (d) Megha, komal

DIRECTION (Q. 9) : Find the mirror image of figures along dotted line MN.

9.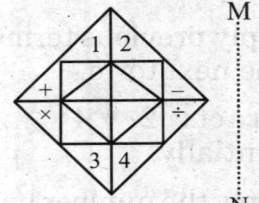

   (a) 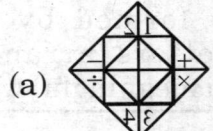 (b)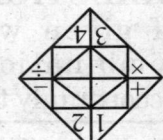

———————— Space for Rough Work ————————

(c)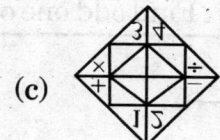

(d)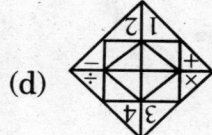

DIRECTION (Q. 10): Find the mirror image of letters combination given below.

10.

(a) ⌐⌐⌠∩I
(b) I∩⌠⌐⌐
(c) L⌐⌠∩I
(d) IU⌠⌐⌐

DIRECTIONS (11 & 12) : Which of the following part is exactly embedded or hidden in figure (X)?

11.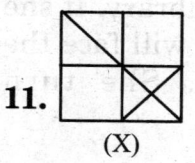
(X)

(a) 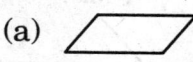 (b)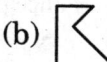

(c) 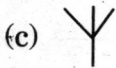 (d)

12.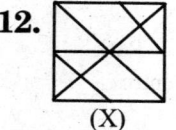
(X)

(a) 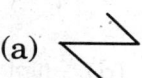 (b)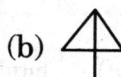

(c) Y (d)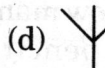

13. Priya walks towards north. After travelling some distance, she turns left. Again after travelling some distance she turns right. In which direction she will be facing now?

(a) North (b) East
(c) West   (d) South

———————— *Space for Rough Work* ————————

14. Megha is facing the library. If she turns to her left, she will face the community centre. She turn _____ to her left.

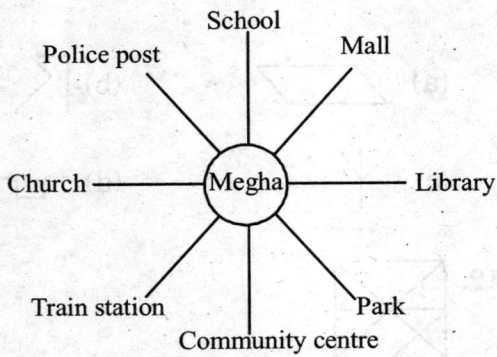

(a) $\frac{1}{4}$ turn (b) $\frac{3}{4}$ turn
(c) $\frac{1}{2}$ turn (d) $\frac{1}{3}$ turn

15. How many possible combinations of 1 pencil and one eraser from 3 pencils and 3 erasers can be formed?

   (a) 10   (b) 9
   (c) 12   (d) 15

16. If today is Friday, 24th February, then previous Friday fell on _____.

   (a) 17th   (b) 16th
   (c) 18th   (d) 19th

DIRECTION (Q. 17): Find odd one out.

17. (a)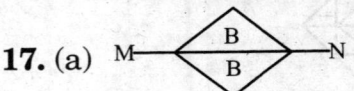
    (b)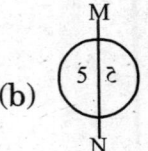
    (c)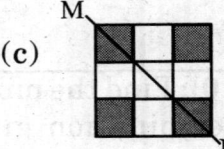
    (d)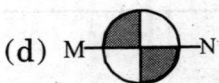

DIRECTION (Q. 18): There is definite relationship between figures (i) and (iii). Establish a similar relationship between figures (ii) and (iv) by selecting a suitable figure from the options that would replace (?) in figure (iv).

18.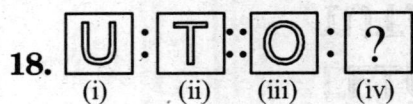

(a)    (b)
(c)    (d)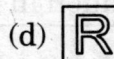

Space for Rough Work

Mock Test-3

19. There are 5 children in a class. Each shook hands with each other. How many handshakes took place?
(a) 12 (b) 18
(c) 10 (d) 5

20. How many horizontal lines are there in the adjoining figure?

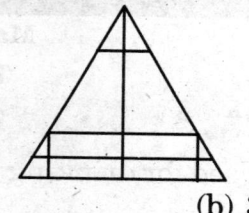

(a) 6 (b) 3
(c) 5 (d) 4

DIRECTIONS (21 to 23) : Read the information carefully and answer the given questions.

Rohit and Kapil are good in Hockey and Volleyball. Sagar and Rohit are good in Hockey and Baseball. Gaurav and Kapil are good in Cricket and Volleyball. Sagar, Gaurav and Mohit are good in football and Baseball.

21. Who is good in Cricket, Volleyball and Hockey?
(a) Kapil (b) Rohit
(c) Sagar (d) Gaurav

22. Who is good in Football, Volleyball, Baseball and Cricket?
(a) Rohit (b) Sagar
(c) Kapil (d) Gaurav

23. Who is good in Hockey and Baseball?
(a) Gaurav (b) Kapil
(c) Sagar (d) Rohit

24. Which of the following diagrams correctly represents Elephants, Wolves, Animals?

25. Choose a figure which would most closely resemble the unfolded form of Figure (Z).

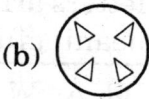

OLYMPIAD Mock Test 4

Name : _____
Number of Questions : 25
Max. Marks : 25
Time : 1 Hour

There is no negative marking in the test.

1. How many circles will be there in Pattern 5?

   Pattern 1   Pattern 2   Pattern 3

   (a) 16 (b) 13
   (c) 14 (d) 7

DIRECTION (Q. 2) : Find the category of given word so formed by combination of letters arranged accordingly to form a meaningful word.

2. R A W E T
   (a) Used in sleeping
   (b) Used for talking
   (c) Used for drinking
   (d) Used for writing

DIRECTION (Q. 3) : Choose one word which can be formed from the letters of the given word.

3. PROGRAMME
   (a) ROAST
   (b) MOARSE
   (c) MORE
   (d) GRAMS

4. If △ means ☐☐ means ◯◯ means ☐ and ☐ means ⌭ then which has exactly four lines of symmetry?

Space for Rough Work

(a) ▢   (b) ○
(c) ▭   (d) △

5. If 2 means 5, 5 means 7 and 7 means 13, then which is prime factor of 45?
(a) 2   (b) 5
(c) 7   (d) 13

DIRECTIONS (Qs. 6 & 7): Eight students are in the queue of Science museum ticket counter. Observe the figure and answer the questions based on it.

6. How many students are behind Garima, if two more students are added in the queue?
(a) 7   (b) 5
(c) 4   (d) 8

7. If Beena and Megha interchange their positions, then Priya is _____ girl behind Beena.
(a) 2nd   (b) 4th
(c) 3rd   (d) 5th

8. There are five friends, Sahil, Ajay, Aman, Raman and Rohit. Ajay is shorter than only one boy. Rohit is shorter than Raman and Aman is taller than Raman but shorter than Ajay. Aman is taller than two boys and shorter than two boys. Who is the tallest?
(a) Ajay
(b) Sahil
(c) Raman
(d) Aman

DIRECTION 9: Find the mirror image of number combination given below.

9. 13579 | Mirror

(a) ୧୮৪31
(b) 6L5E1
(c) ୧୮3E1
(d) 13೭1୧

DIRECTION: Find the mirror image of figures along dotted line MN.

── Space for Rough Work ──

10.

(a) 　(b)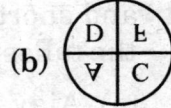

(c) 　(d)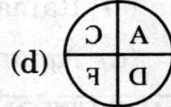

DIRECTIONS (11 & 12) : Which of the following parts is exactly embedded or hidden in figure (X)?

11.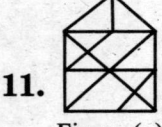
Figure (x)

(a) 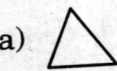　(b)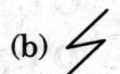

(c) 　(d)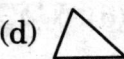

12.

(a) 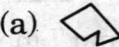　(b)

(c) 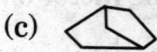　(d)

DIRECTIONS (13 & 14) : Answer the questions based on the direction and places given in the figure.

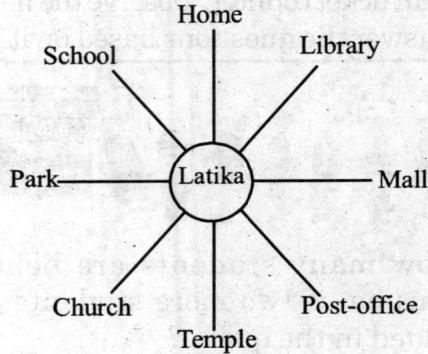

13. Latika is facing home. She will be facing _____, if she makes a $\frac{1}{4}$ turn to her right.
    (a) school　(b) library
    (c) temple　(d) mall

Mock Test-4

14. Latika is facing park. She will be facing _____, if she makes a $\frac{1}{2}$ turn to her left.
   (a) school (b) mall
   (c) temple (d) library

15. How many possible combinations of 1 butterfly and 1 flower can be formed from 3 butterflies and 4 flowers?
   (a) 12 (b) 10
   (c) 11 (d) 9

16. Latika practices her dance competition on every 2nd day of June. 20XX starting from first Monday of month. How many days will she practice for her competition?

June 20XX						
S	M	T	W	Th	F	S
	1					

   (a) 13 days (b) 14 days
   (c) 15 days (d) 16 days

DIRECTION : There is a definite relationship between figures (i) and (iii). Establish a similar relationship between figures (ii) and (iv) by selecting a suitable figure from the options that would replace (?) in figure (iv).

17.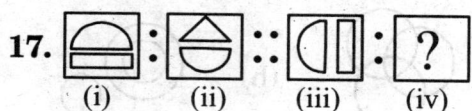

(a) ◁D   (b) ⌒D
(c) ▷D   (d) ◁▷

DIRECTION : Find odd one out.

18. (a) 5   (b) 3
    (c) 2   (d) 8

19. Choose a figure which would most closely resemble the unfolded form of Figure (Z).

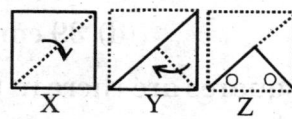

(a) [dots]   (b) [dots]
(c) [dots]   (d) [dots]

—— Space for Rough Work ——

20. Which of the following diagrams correctly represents Sparrows, Birds and Mice.

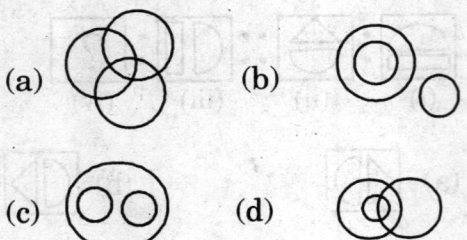

21. What is the height of the rabbit?

(a) 36 cm (b) 37 cm
(c) 38 cm (d) 39 cm

22. How many squares are there in the figure below?

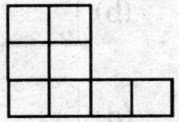

(a) 7 (b) 12
(c) 9 (d) 10

DIRECTIONS (Qs. 23-24) : Read the information carefully and answer the questions.

There are five different houses A to E, in a row. A is to right of B and E is to the left of C and right of A, B is to right of D.

23. Which one of the houses is in the middle of the row?
(a) D (b) A
(c) B (d) C

24. Who sits immediate right of A?
(a) B (b) A
(c) E (d) C

25. The figure X given below is incomplete. Which option figure is required to complete the figure?

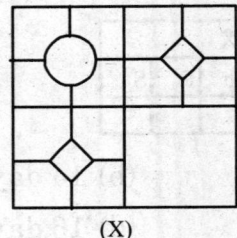

(a) 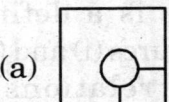 (b)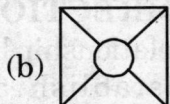

(c)  (d)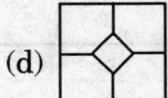

OLYMPIAD
Mock Test

Name : _____ **Max. Marks : 25**
Number of Questions : 25 **Time : 1 Hour**
There is no negative marking in the test.

1. What will be the number on doll 10?

   Doll 1(1), Doll 2(2), Doll 3(3), Doll 4(1), Doll 5(2), Doll 6(3), Doll 7(1), Doll 8(2)

   (a) 2 (b) 1
   (c) 3 (d) 4

2. How many meaningful words could be formed with the third, fifth, fifteenth and seventeenth letter of alphabets given below. If more than two words are formed, give M as the answer, if no such word is formed give X as the answer.

   ABCDEFGHIJKLMNOPQRSTUVWXYZ

   (a) 2 (b) 1
   (c) M (d) X

3. How many possible words could be formed from the letters U, N and R?

   (a) 1 (b) 2
   (c) 3 (d) Zero

4. If VII means XI, XI means XII, XII means C, then which comes immediately after XI in counting?

   (a) XII (b) C
   (c) IX (d) X

5. If △ means ▭, ▭ means ▯ and ▯ means ⊘, then which is formed using squares?

   (a) △ (b) ▭
   (c) ▯ (d) ⊘

Space for Rough Work
---

6. Three persons A, B and C are standing in a queue.

   (i) There are five persons between A and B.

   (ii) There are eight persons between B and C.

   (iii) A is standing behind B.

   If three persons are ahead of C, what could be the number of persons in the queue?

   (a) 19   (b) 17

   (c) 18   (d) 20

DIRECTIONS (Qs. 7 & 8): Answer the questions based on the given series.

A 3 Q R 1 W X P T U I 4 E S 6 V Y Z

7. If 1 and 6 interchange their positions, then how many letters and numbers are there between S and R?

   (a) 10   (b) 9

   (c) 11   (d) 8

8. If all the numbers are removed from the series, then the remaining letters are _____.

   (a) 14   (b) 15

   (c) 16   (c) 13

DIRECTION (Q. 9): Find the mirror image of figures along dotted line MN.

9.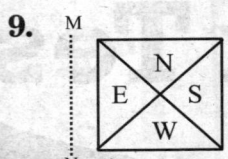

(a)    (b)

(c) 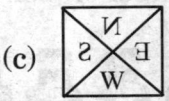   (d)

DIRECTIONS (Qs. 10 & 11): Which of the following parts is exactly embedded or hidden in figure (X)?

10. Figure (X)

(a) 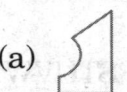   (b)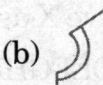

(c)    (d)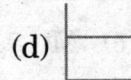

Space for Rough Work

Mock Test-5

11.
Figure (X)

(a) 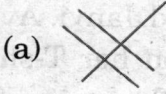 (b)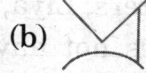

(c) 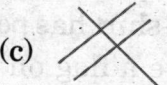 (d)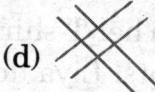

DIRECTIONS (Q. 12 & 13) : Use the diagram below to answer the questions.

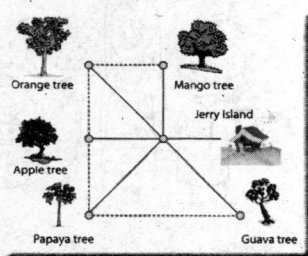

12. Apple tree is _____ of papaya tree.
    (a) north   (b) east
    (c) west   (d) south

13. Jerry faces mango tree, goes straight, take a left turn to reach orange tree, then again a left turn to reach apple tree. At which direction will he face now?

    (a) North   (b) East
    (c) West   (d) South

14. Priya remembers her cousin's birthday falls between 18th March to 21st March. Her father remembers that date is an odd number. What will be the date of Priya's cousin's birthday?

    (a) 19th March
    (b) 20th March
    (c) 21st March
    (d) 18th March

15. How many possible combinations of 1 watch and 1 cell phone can be used from given information?

Watches	Cell phones
Titan	Nokia
Maxima	Motorola
Fastrack	Samsung
Sonata	Tata
	Reliance
	HTC
	Blackberry

(a) 18   (b) 14
(c) 11   (d) 28

Space for Rough Work

DIRECTION (Q. 16) : Which of the following figures is same as the problem Figure?

16.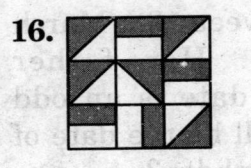

(a) 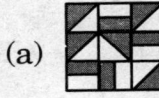   (b)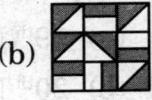

(c)    (d)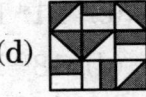

DIRECTION (Q. 17) : There is a definite relatoinship between figures (i) and (iii). Establish a similar relationship between figures (ii) and (iv) by selecting a suitable figure from the options that would replace (?) in figure (iv).

17.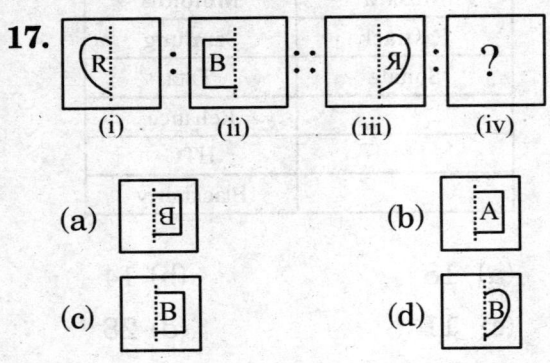

DIRECTION (Qs. 18-19) : Study the following information carefully and answer the questions.

The picture shows Avika and her three sisters, Liya, Bulbul and Janvi. Avika does not have a star on her T-shirt. Bulbul does not have a flower or a flag on her T-shirt. Janvi's T-shirt has polka dots. Liya does not have a flag on her T-shirt.

18. Which sister has flag printed T-shirt?
    (a) Janvi   (b) Avika
    (c) Liya   (d) Bulbul

19. Which sister has star printed T-shirt?
    (a) Bulbul   (b) Janvi
    (c) Avika   (d) Liya

Space for Rough Work

Mock Test-5 LR-27

20. Count the number of triangles in the figure?

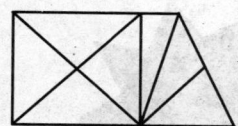

(a) 10 (b) 15
(c) 9 (d) 12

21. Kajal had to solve 9 problems on division for going to museum along with her parents. She took 1 hour 30 minutes to complete the work. Number of minutes she took to solve one problem is _____.

(a) 9 mins (b) 12 mins
(c) 10 mins (d) 8 mins

22. Find the water image of the picture.

(a)

(b)

(c)

(d)

23. Which of the following diagrams correctly represents Boys, Students, Athletes.

(a) 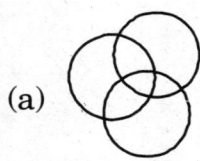 (b)

(c)  (d)

──────── Space for Rough Work ────────

24. Nihal has to wear a shirt, trouser and shoes for an interview. He has the following options available.

Shirt	Trousers	Shoes
Pink	Black	Black
Green	Blue	Brown
White		

How many possible combinations can be made?

(a) 10   (b) 12
(c) 15   (d) 18

25. How many sides does the figure have?

(a) 13   (b) 14
(c) 15   (d) 16

CYBER MOCK TEST 1-3

OLYMPIAD Mock Test 1

Name: _____
Number of Questions : 25
Max. Marks : 25
Time : 1 Hour

There is no negative marking in the test.

1. Zip disks were launched (at the time of its first release) with the capacity of

   (a) 100 MB
   (b) 1 MB
   (c) 1 TB
   (d) 1 GB

2. Which input device can be used to read data from packaging and book covers?

   (a) Optical mark reader
   (b) Keyboard
   (c) Barcode Reader
   (d) Scanner

3. The various parts of computer are connected to each other with

   (a) power cables
   (b) data cables
   (c) fiber cables
   (d) wirelessly

——— *Space for Rough Work* ———

4. Which of the following determines the power of a computer?
   (a) Speed of its processor and capacity of RAM.
   (b) Speed of its processor and capacity of ROM.
   (c) Speed of its operating system and process.
   (d) Only capacity of hard disk.

5. Abacus was the first
   (a) electronic computer
   (b) mechanical computer
   (c) electronic calculator
   (d) mechanical calculator

6. Which generation of computer is still under development?
   (a) Fourth Generation
   (b) Fifth Generation
   (c) Sixth Generation
   (d) Seventh Generation

7. What piece of hardware do EIDE cables connect to?
   (a) Hard disk   (b) CPU
   (c) Keyboard   (d) Mouse

8. What is a peripheral hardware device?
   (a) Any device connected to a computer but not a part of it.
   (b) All websites available on internet.
   (c) All the software running on the computer.
   (d) Paper used in a printer.

9. What is full form of CMOS?
   (a) Complementary metal oxide–semiconductor
   (b) Common metal-oxide-semiconductor.
   (c) Conductance metal-oxide-semiconductor.
   (d) Compact metal-oxide-semiconductor.

———————— Space for Rough Work ————————

Mock Test - 1

10. Which of the following options is/are correct about the software program?

    (a) A set of instructions for your computer

    (b) Type of computer code

    (c) A computer language

    (d) A set of computer code

11. Which of the following is/are software?

    (a)

    (b)

    (c)

    (d) All of these

12. Which of the following is/are system softwares?

    (a) Linux

    (b) Windows 7

    (c) Microsoft Office

    (d) Both (a) and (b)

13. While working with MS-Paint, which option is used to add name to your drawing?

    (a) Text tool

    (b) Pencil tool

    (c) Air brush tool

    (d) Erase tool

Space for Rough Work

14. Which of the following can create an effect that can be used in making an illusion of 3D perspective?

    (a) Skew

    (b) Rotate

    (c) Stretch

    (d) Flip

15. Which of the following tools is/are used to enter the text in your drawing?

    (a) A

    (b) [pencil icon]

    (c) [eraser icon]

    (d) [brush icon]

16. Which of the following is not a social networking site?

    (a) [WhatsApp icon]

    (b) facebook

    (c) LinkedIn

    (d) Google

17. Which of the following is a correct internet address?

    (a) www.yahoo.im

    (b) www.cartoonnetwork.co

    (c) www.hotmail.com

    (d) www.indiatime.comm

18. Which of the following was the name of the first network?

    (a) ARPANET

    (b) EXTRANET

    (c) INTRANET

    (d) ERPANET

———— *Space for Rough Work* ————

19. Which of the following is/are correct about the networking?
    (a) Easy sharing of internet among computers.
    (b) Easy in transfer of data from one computer to another.
    (c) Easy in sharing printers and other devices among connected computers.
    (d) All of these

20. Which of the following is/are computer network that interconnects computers within a limited area such as a residence, school, and laboratory?
    (a) Local Area Network (LAN)
    (b) Metropolitan Area Network (MAN)
    (c) Wide area Network (WAN)
    (d) None of these

21. In MS-Word 2010, which colour wavy line under a word indicates a spelling or grammar mistake?
    (a) Red
    (b) Green
    (c) Yellow
    (d) Both (a) and (b)

22. Microsoft Word 2010 is what type of application software?
    (a) Word processing software
    (b) Word accessing software
    (c) Word writing software
    (d) None of these

———————— Space for Rough Work ————————

23. A pop-up menu is displayed when we right click on a desktop icon. Which of the following options holds the pop-up menu depicted in the given image in Windows 7?

(a)

(b)

(c)

(d)

24. Which of the following is/are correct about windows?
    (a) Windows is an operating system.
    (b) Windows is a programming language.
    (c) Windows is a web-based language.
    (d) Windows is application software.

25. Which of the following is NOT present in control panel?

(a)

(b)

(c)

(d)

OLYMPIAD Mock Test 2

Name: _____
Number of Questions: 25
Max. Marks: 25
Time: 1 Hour

There is no negative marking in the test.

1. The most suitable output device for producing a wage slip printed on a carbonized paper is a/an
   (a) Inject printer
   (b) Laser printer
   (c) Plotter
   (d) Dot matrix printer

2. Identify the given device.

   (a) Flatbed scanner
   (b) Optical flatbed scanner
   (c) Hand-held scanner
   (d) Hand-held sensor

3. Which printer would you recommend to your school administrative department which wants to print out large quantities of black and white mail merged letters?
   (a) Laser
   (b) Inkjet
   (c) Dot matrix
   (d) Daisy-wheel

──────── *Space for Rough Work* ────────

4. Which was the most popular first generation computer?
   (a) IBM 650
   (b) IBM 360
   (c) IBM 1130
   (d) IBM 2700

5. When was the world's first laptop computer introduced in the market and by whom?
   (a) Hewlett-Packard, 1980
   (b) Epson, 1981
   (c) Laplink Traveling Software Inc, 1982
   (d) Tandy Model-200, 1985

6. Why are vacuum tubes also called valves?
   (a) Because they can amplify the weak signals and make them strong
   (b) Because they can stop or allow the flow of current
   (c) Both of the above
   (d) None of the above

7. A tiny piece of silicon which has electric circuits on it is called_____.
   (a) IC chip
   (b) vacuum tube
   (c) memory
   (d) transistor

8. Identify the given device?

   (a) CMOS battery
   (b) NMOS battery
   (c) PMOS battery
   (d) Mobile battery

9. A computer must have_____.
   (a) an Operating System.
   (b) a virus checking program.
   (c) a word processing software.
   (d) a printer attached to them.

10. Which of the following statements is/are correct about the type of software?
    1. Operating system software is independent software.
    2. Application software is dependent on system software.
    3. System software is dependent on Application software.
    (a) (i) and (ii)
    (b) (ii) and (iii)
    (c) (i) and (iii)
    (d) All of these.

11. System software includes.
    (a) device driver
    (b) BIOS
    (c) operating system
    (d) all of these

12. What kind of software coordinates the operations between application software and the computer?
    (a) Utility Software
    (b) System software
    (c) Package software
    (d) Special software

13. Observe the given image.

    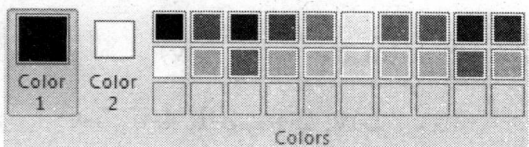

    In this colour 1, colour 2 boxes are used to
    (a) select the foreground colour and Background colour respectively.
    (b) select the background colour and foreground colour respectively.
    (c) both (a) and (b)
    (d) none of these

14. Select the correct match of the following columns, which are related to the MS- Paint.

Column-I	Column-II
1. Copy	i) 🗗
2. Select	ii) ⟲
3. Paste	iii) 📋
4. Resize	iv) 📋
5. Rotate	v) ☐

(a) 1-iv, 2-iii, 3-I, 4-ii, 5-v

(b) 1-ii, 2-iv, 3-i, 4-v, 5-iii

(c) 1-iii, 2-v, 3-iv, 4-i, 5-ii

(d) 1-iv, 2-i, 3-iii, 4-v, 5-ii

15. Which tool should you use to bring a zoomed in or a zoomed out image to its original size?

(a) 🔍+   (b) 🔍−

(c)   (d) 📄

16. Internet is used for audio and video calling across geographies. A popular tool for such internet calls is _____

(a) skype

(b) Google

(c) amazon

(d) ebay

17. Which of the following is a popular website to view video of latest songs and movies?

(a) LinkedIn

(b) facebook

(c) skype

(d) YouTube

———————— *Space for Rough Work* ————————

18. Which of the following software programs is/are used to look at various kinds of internet resources?

    (a) Yahoo

    (b) Google

    (c) Browsers

    (d) You-Tube

19. Who setup the first network?

    (a) Department of defense

    (b) Rubin Balua

    (c) Blaise Pascal

    (d) Roger Benjamin

20. Which of the following is/are the popular networking softwares?

    (a) Windows NT

    (b) MS-windows

    (c) Unix

    (d) All of these

21. Which of the following are an initial and end systems connected to a network?

    (a) Client, host

    (b) PC, server

    (c) Modem, host

    (d) Client, server

Space for Rough Work

22. Which of the following is the default operating system for Macintosh computers?
    (a) Windows
    (b) Mac OS X
    (c) iOS
    (d) Linux OS

23. To select your desktop's background and theme, you should _____
    (a) right click on the desktop and click personalize.
    (b) type personalization in the search bar of the start menu.
    (c) both (a) and (b)
    (d) none of these

24. Which of the following is called the windows preview mode shown in figure given below?

    (a) Shake 3D
    (b) Clip 3D
    (c) Flip 3D
    (d) Peek

Space for Rough Work

25. Select the correct match of the following columns.

Column-I	Column-II
1. System and security	(I) 
2. Network and Internet	(II) 
3. Hardware and sound	(III) 
4. Ease to access center	(IV) 

(a) 1-IV, 2-III, 3-I, 4-II
(b) 1-II, 2-IV, 3-I, 4-III
(c) 1-IV, 2-III, 3-II, 4-I
(d) 1-IV, 2-I, 3-II, 4-III

OLYMPIAD Mock Test 3

Name: _____
Number of Questions : 25

Max. Marks : 25
Time : 1 Hour

There is no negative marking in the test.

1. In which of the following devices, a ball on the top is rolled with a finger to move the cursor on the screen?

    (a)

    (b)

    (c)

    (d)

2. Select the correct match of the following columns.

Column I		Column II
1. Portable hard disk	(i)	
2. Pen drive	(ii)	
3. USB card	(iii)	
4. Memory card reader	(iv)	

--- *Space for Rough Work* ---

(a) 1-iv, 2-iii, 3-i, 4-ii

(b) 1-ii, 2-iv, 3-i, 4-iii

(c) 1-iii, 2-iv, 3-ii, 4-i

(d) 1-iv, 2-i, 3-ii, 4-iii

3. Which of the following is a cloud storage and cloud computing services from apple Inc?

(a) Cloud sync (b) eCloud

(c) mCloud (d) iCloud

4. Which of the following is/are media player and media library application developed by Apple Inc.?

(a) iTunes (b) eTune

(c) mTune (d) Apple Tune

5. Which of the following is a free video chat service from Google that enables both one-on-one chats and group chats with up to ten people at a time?

(a) Google + Trends

(b) Google + Nexus

(c) Google + Next

(d) Google + Hangouts

6. How you can change your desktop's background and aero themes in windows 7?

(a) Right click on the desktop and click personalize or type personalization in the search bar of the start menu.

(b) Select the desktop's background and aero themes as you want.

(c) Both (a) & (b)

(d) None of these

7. Identify the display of given image.

(a) Control panel

(b) Windows Explorer

(c) Desktop

(d) Start menu

8. Identify the icon.

(a) Appearance and Personalization

(b) Computer and mobile

(c) Network and internet

(d) Computer and programs

9. Which feature can you use to combine two or more cells into a single cell?

(a) Insert

(b) Merge

(c) Split

(d) Delete

———————— Space for Rough Work ————————

10. Which of the following can be used in different page format within the same document by separating the differently formatted area?

    (a) Format break

    (b) Line break

    (c) Section break

    (d) Document break

11. The menu system containing the tabs and the commands is called the_____.

    (a) Menu Bar

    (b) System Bar

    (c) Command Prompt

    (d) Ribbon

12. Which of the following is not a type of computer network?

    (a) Local Area Network (LAN)

    (b) Personal Area Network (PAN)

    (c) Wide area Network (WAN)

    (d) Remote Area Network (RAP)

13. Which of the following is/are type of twisted pair cable?

    (a) Coaxial cable

    (b) Shielded Twisted pair

    (c) Unshielded Twisted Pair

    (d) Both (b) & (c)

―――――――――――― Space for Rough Work ――――――――――――

14. Which of the following is correct full form of NIC?

    (a) New Internet Connection

    (b) Network Interface Card

    (c) Network Interface Connection

    (d) Network Internet Connection

15. Which of the following is/are not a search engine?

    (a) Google

    (b) bing

    (c) Yahoo!

    (d) YouTube

16. Which of the following is the set of rules followed in the transmission of information on the internet?

    (a) Internet Policy

    (b) Internet Prime

    (c) Internet Address

    (d) Internet Protocols

17. Which of the following is/are the companies that provide you access to the internet?

    (a) Internet service providers

    (b) Interpol address providers

    (c) Intranet policy providers

    (d) None of these

18. Which of the following options is not used to select the particular section of the image?

———————— Space for Rough Work ————————

Mock Test - 3

C-19

(a) ⬡

(b) ▢

(c) ▣

(d) None of these

19. What is use of invert selection?

(a) It is used to select the particuler part of the image.

(b) It is used to select the reverse portion of the current selection.

(c) It is used to select all portions of the image.

(d) It is used to select the free form selection area.

20. Which of the following steps is correct to change the height and width of the picture?

(a) Image-Resize and Skew-resize

(b) Image-Resize and Skew- Flip vertically

(c) Image-Resize and Skew- Flip horizontally

(d) All of these

21. What type of software is an antivirus software?

(a) Application software

(b) Operating system software

(c) Utility software

(d) None of these

——————— Space for Rough Work ———————

22. Which of the following devices have both the qualities of hardware and software?

    (a) Firmware
    (b) CPU
    (c) UPS
    (d) BIOS

23. Which of the following softwares is used to play music and videos on windows?

    (a) Windows Media Player
    (b) Windows Sync Center
    (c) Windows Sound Recorder
    (d) None of these

24. Which of the following is a latest android operating system version 11.0?

    (a) Marshmallow
    (b) Android-11
    (c) Lollipop
    (d) Kit-Kat

25. Which of the following options is/are correct about phablets?

    (a) They combine the functionality of a tablet and a smartphone.
    (b) They have a screen which is intermediate in size between that of a typical smartphone and a tablet computer.
    (c) Their screen size range varies from 5" to 6.9".
    (d) All of these

─────────── Space for Rough Work ───────────

HINTS & EXPLANATIONS

ENGLISH

MOCK TEST 1

ANSWER KEY

1.	(a)	8.	(c)	15.	(b)	22.	(c)	29.	(b)
2.	(c)	9.	(d)	16.	(b)	23.	(a)	30.	(d)
3.	(b)	10.	(c)	17.	(d)	24.	(a)	31.	(a)
4.	(d)	11.	(a)	18.	(b)	25.	(c)	32.	(b)
5.	(d)	12.	(a)	19.	(a)	26.	(a)	33.	(a)
6.	(c)	13.	(d)	20.	(d)	27.	(a)	34.	(a)
7.	(d)	14.	(b)	21.	(a)	28.	(c)	35.	(a)

1. **(a)** A proper noun has two distinctive features: one, it will name a specific (usually a one-of-a-kind) item, and second, it will begin with a capital letter no matter where it occurs in a sentence. Here, 'Ram' is a proper noun.
2. **(c)** Collective noun is the name we give to a group of nouns to refer to them as one entity.
3. **(b)** A common noun is the word for something (e.g., boy, cat, lake, bridge).
4. **(d)** The verb be takes on different forms in the present and past. Here with the pronoun is plural, so it would take the 'were' form of be.
5. **(d)** A noun that denotes FEMALE SEX is called Feminine Gender. Here with Jolly, the pronoun 'she' will be used.
6. **(c)** We use possessive pronouns to refer to a specific person/people or thing/things (the "antecedent") belonging to a person/people (and sometimes belonging to an animal/animals or thing/things). Here the toys belong to Mandy whose possessive form is 'hers'.
7. **(d)** An adjective is a kind of word that modifies a noun. The adjective gives more information about the noun that goes with it.
8. **(c)** Here the adjective 'red' modifies the noun 'roses'; hence, it is adjective.
9. **(d)** A word or phrase that modifies the meaning of an adjective, verb, or other adverb, expressing manner, place, time, or degree (Example, slowly, there, now, today).

Hints & Explanations

10. **(c)** Here the adverb 'soundly' modifies the verb 'sleep'.
11. **(a)** Prepositions are words that give the additional information to the reader like where something takes place, when or why something takes place and general descriptive information.
12. **(a)** A conjunction is a word used to connect clauses or sentences or to coordinate words in the same clause (Example, and, but, if).
13. **(d)** The conjunction 'because' is used for giving reasons, here having nothing for dinner is the reason for shopping.
14. **(b)** The present tense uses the verb's base form (write, work) or for third-person singular subjects, the base form plus an -s ending (he writes, she works).
15. **(b)** The simple past of 'buy' is 'bought'.
16. **(b)** There are two types of articles: The Definite Article (the) and The Indefinite Article (a and an) because they are used to indicate something unspecific.
17. **(d)** A word or phrase that means exactly or nearly the same as another word or phrase in the same language, here rich is a synonym of wealthy.
18. **(b)** Here centre is the synonym of middle.
19. **(a)** Antonym is a word opposite in meaning to another (here attack and defend).
20. **(d)** The antonym of blunt which means having a broad or rounded end is sharp.
25. **(c)** Ali, Suresh and Anil are proper nouns and they should begin with a capital letter no matter where they occur in the sentence.
26. **(a)** 'What is your full name?' is an interrogative sentence so it should end with the question mark and begin with a capital letter.
27. **(a)** Taj Mahal is located at Agra.
28. **(c)** Taj Mahal was built by Mughal Emperor Shah Jahan.
29. **(b)** It took to build 22 years.
30. **(d)** According to the poem, the cat has the same rights as human beings.
31. **(a)** The poet has drawn a parallel between the rich people and robbers as both rob the innocents.
32. **(b)** Students should conduct themselves in the school by keeping themselves calm and quiet and respecting the teachers.
33. **(a)** A hare, a jackal, an otter and a monkey lived in the forest.
34. **(a)** All the four friends discussed events of the day, exchange advice and made good resolutions every evening.
35. **(a)** On the day of fast, alms were given to beggars or a holy man.

Hints & Explanations

MOCK TEST 2
ANSWER KEY

1.	(b)	8.	(c)	15.	(c)	22.	(a)	29.	(c)
2.	(b)	9.	(a)	16.	(a)	23.	(a)	30.	(d)
3.	(b)	10.	(a)	17.	(b)	24.	(b)	31.	(a)
4.	(c)	11.	(a)	18.	(a)	25.	(a)	32.	(c)
5.	(d)	12.	(c)	19.	(a)	26.	(b)	33.	(a)
6.	(a)	13.	(b)	20.	(a)	27.	(c)	34.	(b)
7.	(a)	14.	(d)	21.	(c)	28.	(d)	35.	(c)

1. **(b)** Any group of fish congregating together is called a shoal.
2. **(b)** The prefix is an element placed at the beginning of a word to adjust or qualify its meaning.
3. **(b)** Hansel and Gretel are in the plural form; hence, will take 'are' of the 'be' form.
4. **(c)** 'His' pronoun is used to refer to a thing or things belonging to or associated with a male person or animal previously mentioned.
5. **(d)** 'We' pronoun is used by a speaker to refer to himself or herself and one or more other people considered together.
6. **(a)** 'Us' pronoun is used by a speaker to refer to himself or herself and one or more other people as the object of a verb or preposition.
7.
8. **(c)** Here black describes the bird that sang beautifully.
9. **(a)** A word or phrase that modifies the meaning of an adjective, verb, or other adverb, expressing manner, place, time, or degree (Example, slowly, there, now, today). Here, once is an adverb.
10. **(a)** The adverb 'always' means at all times; on all occasions.
11. **(a)** The preposition 'at' is used to point out specific time: I will meet you at 10 p.m., The bus will stop here at 6:00 p.m.
12. **(c)** If you say that something will happen in the morning, you mean that it happened or will happen during the morning.
13. **(b)** The conjunction 'but' is used to introduce a phrase or clause contrasting with what has already been mentioned.

Hints & Explanations

14. **(d)** The conjunction 'because' is used for the reason that; since. Example, He went to school on foot because the school bus did not turn up.
15. **(c)** The conjunction 'so' is used as 'and for this reason'; 'therefore'.
16. **(a)** The present tense uses the verb's base form (write, work), or, for third-person singular subjects, the base form plus an -s ending (he writes, she works).
17. **(b)** There are two articles: the and a/an. 'The' is used to refer to specific or particular nouns; a/an is used to modify non-specific or non-particular nouns. An + singular noun beginning with a vowel: an elephant; an egg; an apple; an idiot; an orphan.
18. **(a)** A + singular noun beginning with a consonant: a boy; a car; a bike; a zoo; a dog.
19. **(a)** A word or phrase that means exactly or nearly the same as another word or phrase in the same language, here 'correct' is a synonym of accurate.
20. **(a)** Here praise is a synonym of admire.
21. **(c)** Antonym is a word opposite in meaning to another (here cheap and costly).
22. **(a)** The antonym of famous is unknown.
23. **(a)** Deep means extending relatively far inward while shallow means not deep or strong.
29. **(c)** "Can you speak English?" Is the correct option which begins with the letter in capital and ends with a question mark.
30. **(d)** Coconut oil is used in India as hair oil, cooking oil and body oil.
31. **(a)** Coconut oil is extracted from dried coconut kernel.
32. **(c)** Coconut is fluid at warm temperature but solidifies at cool temperature.
33. **(a)** According to the poem, the pools are bright and deep.
34. **(b)** The hay is thick and green.
35. **(c)** The trout is grey and asleep.

Hints & Explanations

MOCK TEST 3

ANSWER KEY

1.	(a)	8.	(b)	15.	(d)	22.	(b)	29.	(b)
2.	(c)	9.	(d)	16.	(b)	23.	(d)	30.	(d)
3.	(d)	10.	(c)	17.	(c)	24.	(a)	31.	(b)
4.	(c)	11.	(a)	18.	(a)	25.	(b)	32.	(a)
5.	(a)	12.	(b)	19.	(b)	26.	(c)	33.	(a)
6.	(c)	13.	(a)	20.	(b)	27.	(c)	34.	(c)
7.	(d)	14.	(b)	21.	(b)	28.	(a)	35.	(c)

1. **(a)** A noun that denotes a particular thing; usually capitalized. Here, 'Zacob' is the proper noun.
2. **(c)** A noun that denotes any or all members of a class. Here, 'doctor' is the common noun.
3. **(d)** A pronoun that points out an intended referent. Here, 'that' is a demonstrative pronoun.
4. **(c)** Here, 'who' is the interrogative pronoun.
5. **(a)** The present continuous form of shine is shining.
9. **(d)** The preposition 'inside' means internal to, not outside; located in the bounds of, which fits and makes a meaningful sentence.
10. **(c)** The preposition before indicates earlier than in time.
11. **(a)** The preposition by indicates by means of; with aid of; through the act or agency of.
12. **(b)** The conjunction 'because' is used for giving reasons, signifies for the reason that; on account of.
13. **(a)** The conjunction though means even though, in spite of the fact that. Example, Though he is poor, he does not borrow money from anybody.
14. **(b)** The past form of sleep is slept.
15. **(d)** The past participle form of eat is eaten.
16. **(b)** There are two articles: the and a/an. 'The' is used to refer to specific or particular nouns; a/an is used to modify non-specific or non-particular nouns. An + singular noun beginning with a vowel: an elephant; an egg; an apple; an idiot; an orphan.
17. **(c)** Use 'the' to refer to people or objects that are unique. Example, The sun rose at 6:24 this morning. You can go anywhere in the world.
18. **(a)** The present perfect tense is formed with a present tense form of "to have" plus the past participle of the verb (which can be either regular or irregular in form). I have done my job.

19. **(b)** The present perfect of any verb is composed of two elements: the appropriate form of the auxiliary verb to have (present tense), plus the past participle of the main verb.
27. **(c)** Easter is celebrated in Christianity.
28. **(a)** Most religious historians believe that many elements of the Christian observance of Easter were derived from earlier Pagan celebrations.
29. **(b)** According to the Bible, Jesus' death and resurrection occurred around the time of the Jewish Passover, which was celebrated on the first full moon following the vernal equinox.
30. **(d)** An abstract noun is a type of noun that refers to something with which a person cannot physically interact.
31. **(b)** When reflexive pronouns are used to put emphasis on a particular noun, they are called emphatic pronouns. Example, He himself told me this. I finished the job myself.
32. **(a)** We use interrogative pronouns to ask questions. The interrogative pronoun represents the thing that we don't know (what we are asking the question about). There are four main interrogative pronouns: who, whom, what, which.
33. **(a)** We are talking about different places.

MOCK TEST 4

ANSWER KEY

1.	(b)	9.	(d)	17.	(d)	25.	(a)	33.	(b)
2.	(d)	10.	(c)	18.	(b)	26.	(b)	34.	(c)
3.	(d)	11.	(a)	19.	(a)	27.	(d)	35.	(b)
4.	(b)	12.	(a)	20.	(c)	28.	(a)	36.	(a)
5.	(a)	13.	(c)	21.	(d)	29.	(a)	37.	(d)
6.	(b)	14.	(a)	22.	(b)	30.	(a)	38.	(a)
7.	(d)	15.	(c)	23.	(b)	31.	(a)	39.	(d)
8.	(c)	16.	(a)	24.	(d)	32.	(c)	40.	(c)

1. **(b)** Material Noun is the name of a material or a substance or an ingredient of an alloy. Example: Cotton dress is cheap.
2. **(d)** A common noun is the word for something (Example, bird, boy, cat, lake, bridge).
3. **(d)** Collective noun is the name we give to a group of nouns to refer to them as one entity. Example, a bunch of keys.
4. **(b)** Past tense of shine is shone.

Hints & Explanations

5. **(a)** We use between to refer to two things which are clearly separated. We use among to talk about things which are not clearly separated because they are part of a group or crowd or mass of objects.
6. **(b)** Prepositions of time: at, in, on. We use: at for a precise time, in for months, years, centuries and long periods, on for days and dates.
7. **(d)** That introduces a subordinate clause expressing a statement or hypothesis. Example, She said that she was disappointed.
8. **(c)** Past tense of grow is grew.
9. **(d)** Past participle form of take is taken.
10. **(c)** The rule about a/an is based on the sound of the beginning of the following word, not on its first letter. The first sound of one is "w" even though it begins with the vowel "o". Therefore, the indefinite article must be "a" not "an".
11. **(a)** The past tense is a grammatical tense whose principal function is to place an action or situation in past time. Here the verb meet becomes met in past tense.
12. **(a)** The past form of sink is sank.
13. **(c)** We use the Present Perfect Continuous to show that something started in the past and has continued up until now. Example, They have been waiting here for two hours.
23. **(b)** Tail, beak, head are all nouns but tell is a verb.
24. **(d)** Material Noun is the name of a material or a substance or an ingredient of an alloy. Examples: Bangles are made of gold.
25. **(a)** An abstract noun is a type of noun that refers to something with which a person cannot physically interact. Example, beauty, bravery, brilliance, brutality, etc.
26. **(b)** A relative pronoun is used to connect a clause or phrase to a noun or pronoun. Example, who, whom, which, whoever, whomever, whichever, and that.
27. **(d)** The verb trudge, swam and wait do not fit in the sentence.
28. **(a)** In the sentence, nice, police and dry do not fit but large is an appropriate word.
29. **(a)** The coordinating conjunction "and" is used to link different parts of the sentence, which is the main job of conjunctions. Basically, conjunctions join words, phrases and clauses together. Coordinating Conjunctions are and, but, or, nor, for, yet, so.
30. **(a)** The coordinating conjunction "and" will be used to link different parts of the sentence.
31. **(a)** The preposition 'in' is used for months - in July, in September, for year- in 1998, in 2014, for seasons- in summer, in the summer of 72.
32. **(c)** The preposition 'by' is used to indicate a mean or method. Example, Please send this package to Mumbai by airmail, I came here by train.

33. **(b)** The Golden Gate Park is the proper noun and park is common noun.
34. **(c)** The object pronoun of Henry is him.
35. **(b)** The present tense uses the verb's base form (go, play) or for third-person singular subjects, the base form plus an -s ending (he goes, she plays).
36. **(a)** Negatives in the simple present are formed by adding don't or doesn't before the simple form of the verb.
37. **(d)** Sentences that ask a question are called interrogative sentences. They're easy to spot -they always end with a question mark (?).
38. **(a)** An exclamatory sentence is a sentence that expresses great emotion such as excitement, surprise, happiness and anger, and ends with an exclamation point.
39. **(d)** The meaning of preposition UNLIKE is: not like: as a: marked by lack of resemblance: different. The two books are quite unlike. b : marked by inequality : unequal. Hence, the opposite of sturdy is fragile.
40. **(c)** We usually use but as a conjunction linking two contrastive sentences or clauses. Example, they had very little money, but (they) always bought their children expensive toys.

MOCK TEST 5

ANSWER KEY

1.	(d)	9.	(b)	17.	(b)	25.	(b)	33.	(b)
2.	(b)	10.	(a)	18.	(d)	26.	(b)	34.	(d)
3.	(c)	11.	(c)	19.	(c)	27.	(b)	35.	(a)
4.	(d)	12.	(b)	20.	(c)	28.	(a)	36.	(b)
5.	(b)	13.	(c)	21.	(d)	29.	(a)	37.	(a)
6.	(c)	14.	(d)	22.	(a)	30.	(b)	38.	(d)
7.	(b)	15.	(b)	23.	(d)	31.	(b)	39.	(c)
8.	(c)	16.	(a)	24.	(c)	32.	(c)	40.	(b)

1. **(d)** Dancer, painter, singer are all nouns but hotter is an adjective.
2. **(b)** Belt, shoe, lace are all nouns but black is an adjective.
3. **(c)** A relative pronoun is used to connect a clause or phrase to a noun or pronoun. Example, who, whom, which, whoever, whomever, whichever, and that.
4. **(d)** The students who were absent... is the correct answer as the who acts as a relative pronoun.

Hints & Explanations

5. **(b)** The ducks swim in the pond is correct option.
6. **(c)** Only police officers can create road barrier; hence, police is the correct fill-in.
7. **(b)** The conjunction 'but' is used to introduce a phrase or clause contrasting with what has already been mentioned.
8. **(c)** The conjunction 'or' is used to express possibilities. Example,
   - Is it Tuesday or Wednesday today?
   - You can pay now or when you come back to pick up the paint.
   - Are you listening to me or not?
9. **(b)** The preposition 'on' is used on a surface of something or in a particular place.
   He is on the phone right now. She has been on the computer since this morning. My favourite movie will be on TV tonight.
10. **(a)** The preposition 'for' here is used to mean because of. Example, I am so happy for you. We feel deeply sorry for your loss, For this reason, I've decided to quit this job.
11. **(c)** The preposition 'in' here is used to express while doing something. Example, In preparing for the final report, we revised the tone three times, Advertising needs to be impressive in marketing a product.
12. **(b)** She hugged both her mom and dad.
13. **(c)** The common noun in the sentence is fruit while the proper noun is apples and oranges.
14. **(d)** Foreign Language Club is the proper noun while club is common noun.
15. **(b)** The object pronoun of 'Kris and his dad' is 'them'.
16. **(a)** In the simple present, with third person singular, the verb always ends in -s
    He wants, she needs, he gives, she thinks.
17. **(b)** Negatives in the simple present are formed by adding don't or doesn't before the simple form of the verb. The baby doesn't sleep at night. I don't like mangoes.
18. **(d)** A complete sentence must have a subject and predicate. A predicate is a verb that expresses the subject's action or state of being.
19. **(c)** Captivity means the state of being imprisoned or slave; freedom is the condition of being free.
20. **(c)** Reveal means make visible and cover means provide with a covering or cause to be covered.
21. **(d)** Huge means unusually great in size or amount or degree or especially extent or scope and giant also means anything of exceptional size.
22. **(a)** The baby sheep is also known as lamb.
23. **(d)** Nuts and bolts means detailed practical information about how something works or how something can be accomplished.

Hints & Explanations

24. **(c)** The idiomatic phrase 'on the tip of one's tongue', means a thought or idea is about to be said or almost remembered. Example, I have his name right on the tip of my tongue.
25. **(b)** Suddenly, without warning.
26. **(b)** They are going to help us. (subject+ aux.verb+ verb+ to-infinitive+object)
27. **(b)** John washed the car yesterday. (subject+verb+object+adverb).
28. **(a)** Most bats are harmless to people. (subject+ aux.verb+ adjective+ preposition+ noun)
29. **(a)** You can only be confident about the goals which you set for yourself.
30. **(b)** Tall is in contrast with 'short', hence, the correct option.
31. **(b)** Telling something to friends or revealing a secret is in contrast with something meant to be secret.
32. **(c)** Lily felt overjoyed about living in her new town.
33. **(b)** The passage is mainly about Lily and the four seasons, i.e., winter, spring, summer and autumn.
34. **(d)** All the four seasons is Lily's favourite thing in the new town.
35. **(a)** In addition means also, as well.
36. **(b)** In the passage, Lily as well as the four seasons have been described.
37. **(a)** It snows in her new town, hence option I.
38. **(d)** In paragraph 5, we learn about the costumes that Lilly likes to wear. The author writes, "Last year she wore a mouse costume. This year she will wear a fish costume". Using this information, we can understand that Lilly likes to wear animal costumes. Therefore, it makes sense that she would wear a bird costume next year. Choice (d) is correct. The passage does not provide information to support choices (a), (b), and (c). Therefore, they are incorrect.
39. **(c)** Autumn is also called 'fall'.
40. **(b)** Commas are used to separate the individual words or phrases that together make up a list. Ex- The fish kept in the ponds were eels, tench, pike, perch and carp.

MATHEMATICS

MOCK TEST-1

ANSWERS KEY

1.	(b)	8.	(a)	15.	(c)	22.	(d)	29.	(c)
2.	(b)	9.	(c)	16.	(a)	23.	(d)	30.	(c)
3.	(c)	10.	(b)	17.	(b)	24.	(a)	31.	(b)
4.	(a)	11.	(c)	18.	(a)	25.	(b)	32.	(d)
5.	(c)	12.	(c)	19.	(b)	26.	(c)	33.	(b)
6.	(a)	13.	(b)	20.	(b)	27.	(b)	34.	(b)
7.	(d)	14.	(b)	21.	(b)	28.	(b)	35.	(b)

1. **(b)** Twice of 986456 = 1972912
   $\therefore$ Required number
   = 1972912 − 563876
   = 1409036

2. **(b)** 57 − 7 = 50 and 67 − 7 = 60

   $$50\overline{)60}\,(1$$
   $$\underline{50}$$
   $$10\overline{)50}\,(5$$
   $$\underline{50}$$
   $$\times$$

   HCF of 50 and 60 = 10
   Hence, 10 is the greatest number that divides 57 and 67 leaving remainder 7.

3. **(c)** 985 = 900 + 50 + 10 + 10 + 10 + 5
   CM + L + X + X + X + V
   CMLXXXV

4. **(a)** 42 = 2 × 3 × 7
   70 = 2 × 5 × 7
   Common factor = 2 × 7 = 14

5. **(c)** (A) → 3, (B) → 4, (C) → 1, (D) → 2

6. **(a)** 3rd number from the left is 7
   7 − 2 = 5
   5 is 1st number from right.

7. **(d)** Anjali put 50 pickles on 10 sandwiches.
   Number of pickles on one sandwich = 50 ÷ 10 = 5

8. **(a)** $\dfrac{5}{2}, \dfrac{5}{7}, \dfrac{5}{9}$ and $\dfrac{5}{3}$ are unlike fractions.

9. **(c)** One small rectangle contains 2 equal triangles.
   Total number of triangles
   = 2 × 16 = 32
   Number of shaded triangles
   = 16
   Number of unshaded triangles
   = 32 − 16 = 16
   Fraction = $\dfrac{16}{32} = \dfrac{1}{2}$

10. **(b)** Sum of ages of Raghu and Kavita = 21 + 22 = 43 years
    43 = 40 + 3
    = XL + III
    = XLIII

11. **(c)** Place value of 9 at thousands place = 9,000

Hints & Explanations

Place value of 9 at tens place
= 90
Product = 9000 × 90
= 8,10,000.

12. **(c)** 5 + 6 = 11
Carry 1 is given to tens place
6 + 1 + ☐ = 15
7 + ☐ = 15
☐ = 15 – 7 = 8.

13. **(b)** ?⃝ + 7 = ◇20
?⃝ = 20 – 7 = 13
Now, ?⃝ – 5 = 13
?⃝ = 13 + 5 = 18
Now, ?⃝ – 10 = 18
?⃝ = 18 + 10 = 28

14. **(b)** AC + DE + GJ = 2 cm + 1 cm + 3 cm = 6 cm
From the given options
BH = 6 cm.

15. **(c)** 4 : 15 p.m. = 16 : 15 hours
Now,

Hours	Minutes
16	15
+ 1	28
17	43

17 : 43 hours = 5 : 43 p.m.

16. **(a)** Number of books in 5 shelves
= 5 × 12 = 60
Total number of books
= 60 + 9 = 69.

17. **(b)** Perimeter of rectangle
= 2 × (length + breadth)
A triangle having all its sides different is a scalene triangle.

18. **(a)** ∠BCA = 78°
78° is an acute angle.

19. **(b)** Area of square = 9 × 9 = 81 cm^2
Area of rectangle
= 11 × 7 = 77 cm^2
Square encloses more area.

20. **(b)** Cube has 6 faces. Each face is a square of same size. It has 8 vertices and 12 edges.

21. **(b)** Length of boundary of park means perimeter of park.

22. **(d)** Length of boundary of shaded shape = 18 cm
Therefore perimeter of shaded part = 18 cm

23. **(d)** Diameter

24. **(a)** (4 + 5 + 8 + ?) = 23
17 + ? = 23
? = 6 cm

25. **(b)** Arrow in fig. B is in opposite direction to that in fig. A.

26. **(c)** First prime odd number = 3.
So, diameter = 2 × 3 = 6 units.

27. **(b)** 500 g of apple costs = ₹ 50
1 g of apple costs = ₹ $\dfrac{50}{500}$
1 kg of apple costs
= $\dfrac{50}{500}$ × 1000 = ₹ 100

Hints & Explanations

28. **(b)** Amount of water in vessel P
 = 20 ml
 Amount of water in vessel Q
 = 160 ml
 Amount of water in R
 = 20 + 160 = 180 ml
 = 0.18 litre

29. **(c)** In 18 litres of petrol, bus runs
 = 234 km
 In 1 litre of petrol, bus runs
 $= \dfrac{234}{18} = 13$ km
 In 45 litres of petrol bus runs
 13 × 45 = 585 km

Sol. (Qs. 30 to 33):

30. **(c)** Number of students participated in the competition
 = 30 + 50 + 10 + 60 + 20 + 30
 = 200.

31. **(b)** 1 cm = 10 students

32. **(d)** 60

33. **(b)** In class I and VI, 30 students participated in the competition from each class.

34. **(b)** One box will increase in next figure.

35. **(b)** 3 × 2 = 6, 6 × 2 = 12,
 12 × 2 = 24 24 × 2 = 48,
 48 × 2 = 96

MOCK TEST-2

ANSWERS KEY

1.	(d)	8.	(a)	15.	(c)	22.	(b)	29.	(a)
2.	(a)	9.	(b)	16.	(c)	23.	(b)	30.	(c)
3.	(d)	10.	(c)	17.	(d)	24.	(b)	31.	(c)
4.	(c)	11.	(c)	18.	(a)	25.	(b)	32.	(b)
5.	(b)	12.	(c)	19.	(d)	26.	(c)	33.	(a)
6.	(b)	13.	(c)	20.	(a)	27.	(a)	34.	(c)
7.	(b)	14.	(b)	21.	(c)	28.	(c)	35.	(a)

1. **(d)** Part of wall painted blue and green $= \dfrac{1}{3} + \dfrac{2}{7}$
 $= \dfrac{7+6}{21} = \dfrac{13}{21}$
 Part of wall painted yellow
 $= 1 - \dfrac{13}{21} = \dfrac{21-13}{21} = \dfrac{8}{21}$

2. **(a)** 0.00009 + 0.007 + 0.05 + 0.4
 = 0.45709

3. **(d)** 34 × second number = 476
 Second number $= \dfrac{476}{34} = 14$

4. **(c)** Total distance covered in two days = 12 km
 Distance covered on first day
 = 7½ km

Hints & Explanations

Distance covered on second day

$= 12 - 7½ \left(12 - \dfrac{15}{2}\right)$ km

$= 4½$ km

5. **(b)** Total money = ₹ 435 + ₹ 200
    = ₹ 635

6. **(b)** Number of children in each row
    $= \dfrac{161}{7} = 23$

7. **(b)** Except fig (b), other figures do not have equal areas.

8. **(a)** Total number of small squares
    $= 10 \times 10 = 100$

    $\dfrac{1}{4}$ th of total small squares

    $= \dfrac{1}{4} \times 100 = 25$

    Shaded squares = 18
    Number of squares shaded in order to have 25 figure
    Shaded = 25 − 18 = 7

9. **(b)** 1 + .1 + .01 + .001 = 1.111

10. **(c)** Shaded part $= 0.03 = \dfrac{3}{100}$

    Unshaded part $= \dfrac{100-3}{100} = \dfrac{97}{100}$

    ∴ 97 parts out of 100 is unshaded.

11. **(c)** If we shade square 3, figure will be symmetrical.

12. **(c)** (A) → 2, (B) → 4, (C) → 1, (D) → 3

13. **(c)** Length of boundary of figure = 42 cm

14. **(b)** Perimeter = 7 + 7 + 7 + 7 + 7 + 7 + 7 + 7 = 56 cm

15. **(c)** Perimeter $= \dfrac{1}{4} \times 56$ cm = 14 cm
    fig (c) has 14 cm perimeter

16. **(c)** Height of flag = 10 − 1 = 9 units

17. **(d)** Distance covered in 1 round
    = Perimeter of park
    Perimeter of park
    = 66 m + 75 m + 102 m + 85 m
    = 328 m

18. **(a)** Perimeter of figure given in option (a) is longest.
    fig (a) → 4 × 6 = 24 cm
    fig (b) → 10 + 10 + 3 = 23 cm
    fig (c) → 2 (8 + 2) = 20 cm
    fig (d) → 2 (7 + 4) = 22 cm

19. **(d)** Area of square
    $= 20 \times 20 = 400$ cm^2
    Area of rectangle
    = Area of square
    ? × 25 = 400
    $? = \dfrac{400}{25} = 16$ cm

20. **(a)** A polygon made of 4 straight lines is called a quadrilateral.

21. **(c)** 1 kg = 1000 g
    0.5 kg = 500 g
    1.5 kg = (1000 + 500) g = 1500 g

22. **(b)** 1 kg + 500 g + 500 g = 2 kg
    1 kg + 500 g + 250 g + 250 g
    = 2 kg

Hints & Explanations

1 kg + 500 g + 250 g + 100 g + 100 g + 50 g = 2 kg

23. (b) Sumanth was (1993 − 1976) = 17 years old in 1993.

24. (b) A : V, L and D are never repeated or subtracted.

B : Adding 1 to a number gives its successor.

25. (b) Dividend = (Quotient × Divisor) + Remainder
= (35 × 23) + 21
= 805 + 21 = 826

26. (c) Cost of 3 umbrellas = ₹ 960

Cost of 1 umbrella

$= \dfrac{960}{3} = ₹\ 320$

Cost of 2 hats
= 720 − 320 = ₹ 400

Cost of 1 hat

$= \dfrac{400}{2} = ₹\ 200$

27. (a) Height of tallest child = 105 cm
Height of shortest child = 60 cm
Difference = 105 cm − 60 cm
= 45 cm

Sol. (28 to 30):

28. (c) 5 toys more than Samrat
= 5 + 25 = 30
Aman has 30 toys.

29. (a) 2 times as many as Raj has
= 2 × 15 = 30 toys.
Aman has 30 toys.

30. (c) Total toys
= 35 + 25 + 30 + 15 = 105

31. (c) All other figures have half part shaded.

32. (b) 5 × 5 = 25
25 × 5 = 125
125 × 5 = 625
In fourth year, company has 625 employes.

33. (a) In both ways Riya is counted two times.
Number of students in queue
= (17 + 19) − 1 = 35

34. (c) 8 × 4 = 32; 8 × 5 = 40
8 × 8 = 64; 8 × $\boxed{7}$ = 56

35. (a) 5 $\xrightarrow{+3}$ 8 $\xrightarrow{-1}$ 7 $\xrightarrow{+3}$ 10 $\xrightarrow{-1}$ 9 $\xrightarrow{+3}$ 12 $\xrightarrow{-1}$ 11 $\xrightarrow{+3}$ $\boxed{14}$

Hints & Explanations

MOCK TEST-3

ANSWERS KEY

1.	(b)	8.	(b)	15.	(b)	22.	(b)	29.	(b)
2.	(d)	9.	(c)	16.	(b)	23.	(d)	30.	(c)
3.	(b)	10.	(a)	17.	(b)	24.	(a)	31.	(d)
4.	(c)	11.	(b)	18.	(a)	25.	(c)	32.	(a)
5.	(a)	12.	(d)	19.	(a)	26.	(c)	33.	(d)
6.	(d)	13.	(d)	20.	(b)	27.	(c)	34.	(c)
7.	(d)	14.	(b)	21.	(b)	28.	(a)	35.	(d)

1. (b) $0.0003 + 0.004 + 0.07 + 0.9 + 7$
    $= 7.9743$

2. (d)
   ```
            200
          /    \
        80      120
       /  \    /  \
      30   50    70
     / \  / \  / \
    10 20 30  40
   ```

3. (b) XLIII = 43
    48 − 43 = 5
    5 = V should be inserted between L and I.

4. (c) $7432 − 671 × 3 + 3261$
    $= 10693 − 2013$
    $= 8680$

5. (a) $6 + 6 + 6 + ...$ 695 times
    $= 6 × 695 = 4170$

6. (d) $3984 ÷ \dot{8} = 4\boxed{9}8$

7. (d) $A × 59 = 322376$
    $A = 322376 ÷ 59$
    $A = 5464$

8. (b) (A) → 3, (B) → 1, (C) → 4, (D) → 2

9. (c) 0.003
    $= \dfrac{3}{1000}$ → three - thousandth

10. (a) $623.523 = 623.52300$

11. (b)

hours	minutes	seconds
2	45	23
+3	35	53
5	80	76

    5 hrs 80 min 76 sec.
    = 5 hrs (60 + 20) min. (60 + 16) sec
    = (5 + 1) hrs (20 + 1) min. 16 sec.
    = 6 hrs 21 min 16 sec.

12. (d) Fraction reprsented by shaded region = $\dfrac{1}{4}$
    which is same as in option (d)

13. (d) $0.36 − 0.6 = 0.30$

14. (b) KM = 8.4 cm
    KL = KM − LM
    $= 8.4$ cm $− 3.3$ cm $= 5.1$ cm
    KN + LN = 5.1 cm + 7.5 cm
    = 12.6 cm

15. (b) L.C.M. of 2, 5 and 8
    ```
    2 | 2, 5, 8
      | 1, 5, 4
    ```
    $= 2 × 5 × 4 = 40$

Hints & Explanations

16. (b) L.C.M. of 11 and 13

$$\begin{array}{r|rr} 11 & 11, & 13 \\ 13 & 1, & 13 \\ \hline & 1, & 1 \end{array}$$

L.C.M. of 11 and 13
$= 11 \times 13 = 143$
$\therefore \quad ? = 4$

17. (b) B : A ray has no fixed length.
D : Two radii of a circle are of same length.

18. (a) Perimeter of rectangle
$= 2(8 + 4) = 24$ cm
Perimeter of rectangle
= perimeter of square
$4 \times$ side $= 24$ cm
side $= \dfrac{24}{4} = 6$ cm

19. (a) Angle between 0° and 90° is known as acute angle.

20. (b) Isosceles triangles has two equal sides.

21. (b) 2

22. (b) 0.9 is the greatest among all options.

23. (d) AB = ED = CD = BC = 5cm
Perimeter of the figure
= AB + BC + CD + DE + EA
= 5 + 5 + 5 + 5 + 5 = 25 cm
(BE is not included because this line is inside the figure).

24. (a) Total distance travelled
= 75 km 800 m + 1800 km 40 m
= 1875 km 840 m

25. (c) Total bill = ₹ (720 + 950 + 25)
= ₹ 1920
He will get back = ₹ (2000 – 1920)
= ₹ 80

Sol. (26 to 28):

26. (c) Cost of 2 soups = 2 × 300
= ₹ 600

27. (c) Cost of 2 packet of chips
= 2 × 100 = ₹ 200
Cost of 1 pizza = ₹ 370
Cost of 2 juices = 2 × 100 = ₹ 200
Total cost = ₹ (200 + 370 + 200)
= ₹ 770

28. (a) Cost of 5 cups of tea
= ₹ 5 × 80 = ₹ 400
Cost of 1 pizza = ₹ 370
Total cost = ₹ (370 + 400) = ₹ 770

29. (b) 1 is neither composite nor prime becasue it has only one factor that is 1.

30. (c) 4 : 15 – 3 : 50 = 25 minutes

31. (d)

32. (a)

33. (d)

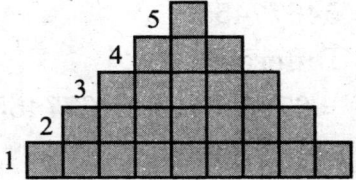

34. (c) $\bigcirc \times \bigcirc = 100$
$10 \times 10 = 100$
$\bigcirc = 10$
$2 \triangledown = 120 - 10 = 110$
$\triangledown = \dfrac{110}{2} = 55$
$? = 55 - 10 = 45$

35. (d) Number of complete squares = 26
Number of half squares = 6
Area of shaded parts
$= 26 + \dfrac{6}{2} = 29$ cm^2

MOCK TEST-4

ANSWERS KEY

1.	(d)	9.	(d)	17.	(d)	25.	(a)	33.	(c)
2.	(a)	10.	(c)	18.	(a)	26.	(b)	34.	(b)
3.	(b)	11.	(b)	19.	(d)	27.	(b)	35.	(c)
4.	(a)	12.	(a)	20.	(b)	28.	(c)	36.	(c)
5.	(d)	13.	(a)	21.	(b)	29.	(d)	37.	(b)
6.	(a)	14.	(d)	22.	(a)	30.	(c)	38.	(b)
7.	(d)	15.	(b)	23.	(b)	31.	(a)	39.	(d)
8.	(b)	16.	(c)	24.	(a)	32.	(a)	40.	(a)

1. **(d)** LXIV = 64, LXVI = 66,
   CLI = 151
   CXXXVII = 137
   151 > 137 > 66 > 64

2. **(a)** Successor of 67854398 is 67854399
   Predecessor of 54677456 is 54677455
   Difference
   = 67854399 − 54677455
   = 13176944

3. **(b)** A + B + 45896 = C + D
   A + B + 45896 = 96023 + B
   A = 96023 + B − 45896 − B
   A = 50127

4. **(a)** 24 + 16 − 10 − 2 + 15
   = 40 + 15 − 10 − 2
   = 55 − 10 − 2
   = 45 − 2 = 43

5. **(d)** Dividend = Divisor × Quotient + Remainder
   A = B × C + D

6. **(a)** Unit fraction = $\dfrac{1}{8}$
   We have to shade one part out of eight.

7. **(d)** He shade 3 part out of every 10 part
   In total he shade 3 × 10 = 30 part
   Shaded fraction = $\dfrac{30}{100}$

8. **(b)** In figure (i), 7 part is shaded out of 12
   In figure (ii), total squares = 24
   $\dfrac{\text{shaded box}}{24} = \dfrac{7}{12}$
   shaded box = $\dfrac{7}{12} \times 24 = 14$

9. **(d)** $\dfrac{1}{15} + \dfrac{2}{15} + ? = \dfrac{1}{15} + \dfrac{5}{15} + \dfrac{5}{15}$
   $\dfrac{3}{15} + ? = \dfrac{1+5+5}{15} = \dfrac{11}{15}$
   $? = \dfrac{11}{15} - \dfrac{3}{15} = \dfrac{8}{15}$

Hints & Explanations

10. **(c)** X = 10, L = 50
    L − X = 50 − 10 = 40
    X can be subtracted from L.
    X can be repeated maximum 3 times.

11. **(b)** $\dfrac{1}{4} + \dfrac{3}{4}$

12. **(a)** Fraction represented by gold fish = $\dfrac{5}{4+5+1} = \dfrac{5}{10}$

13. **(a)** True

14. **(d)** 84,551 > 84,503 > 80,968

15. **(b)** 5638 − 21 ☐ 9 = 3449
    5638 − 3449 = 2189 = 21 ☐ 9

16. **(c)** (A) → 4, (B) → 1, (C) → 2, (D) → 3

17. **(d)** $\dfrac{1}{7} + \dfrac{2}{7} + \dfrac{\square}{7} = 1\dfrac{3}{7}$
    $\dfrac{3}{7} + \dfrac{\square}{7} = \dfrac{10}{7}$
    $\dfrac{3+\square}{7} = \dfrac{10}{7}$
    ⇒ Number in place of ☐ should be 7.

18. **(a)** Fraction of cake left
    $= \dfrac{12-9}{12} = \dfrac{3}{12}$

19. **(d)**

20. **(b)** Acute angle

21. **(b)** Multiples of 10 from 20 to 150 are 20, 30, 40, 50, 60, 70, 80, 90, 100, 110, 120, 130, 140 and 150

22. **(a)** Because it has two equal sides.

23. **(b)** Sum of angles of a triangle is 180°.

24. **(a)** Length of small farm land
    $= \dfrac{350}{2} = 175$ m
    Width of small farm land
    $= \dfrac{150}{2} = 75$ m
    Perimeter
    = 2(175 + 75) = 500 m

25. **(a)** In a right angled triangle, one angle measures 90° and other two angles are acute angles.

26. **(b)** BC is not the diameter of circle

27. **(b)** 42 − 7 = 35 and 67 − 7 = 60
    To find H.C.F. of 35 and 60

    ```
    35) 60 (1
        35
        ──
        25) 35 (1
            25
            ──
            10) 25 (2
                20
                ──
                5) 10 (2
                   10
                   ──
                    ×
    ```

    Hence, 5 is the greatest number that divides 42 and 67 leaving 7 as remainder.

28. **(c)** 42 ÷ 7 × 5 + 4 − 9
    = 6 × 5 + 4 − 9
    = 30 + 4 − 9
    = 34 − 9 = 25

29. **(d)** Distance between two dots
    $= \dfrac{14}{14}$ cm = 1 cm
    Length of rope needed for border Y
    = 24 × 1 cm = 24 cm

30. **(c)** Water in vessel P = 20 ml
    Water in vessel Q = 250 ml
    Water in vessel R
    = (250 + 20)
    = 270 ml = 0.27 l

20

Hints & Explanations

31. (a) If length of branch = 210 cm
Length of each stump
$= \dfrac{210}{3} = 70$ cm

32. (a) Total amount spend on marketing
$= 2 \times 10.5 + 3 \times 25.50 + 34.75$
$= 21 + 76.50 + 34.75$
$= ₹ 132.25$

33. (c) The distance between the shopping mall and Rehaan's house = 3 km 535 m = 3535 m

34. (b) 17 : 10 hours − 25 minutes
= 16 : 45 hours
= 4 : 45 p.m

35. (c) $5 + 5.01 + 51.051 + 515.515$
$= 576.576$

36. (c) $(28 - 10 - 6) + 1 = 13$ Feb
28 February is counted. Therefore, we have to add 1.

37. (b) $5 \times \Box = 3000$
$\Box = \dfrac{3000}{5} = 600$

38. (b) As $\Box$ represents 600 employees
$\dfrac{5400}{600} = 9$

In $\Box$ represents the numbers of employees in Mumbai.

39. (d)

40. (a)

MOCK TEST-5

ANSWERS KEY

1.	(b)	9.	(c)	17.	(a)	25.	(b)	33.	(c)
2.	(a)	10.	(b)	18.	(b)	26.	(c)	34.	(a)
3.	(a)	11.	(b)	19.	(c)	27.	(c)	35.	(c)
4.	(b)	12.	(c)	20.	(d)	28.	(b)	36.	(c)
5.	(c)	13.	(b)	21.	(c)	29.	(a)	37.	(c)
6.	(a)	14.	(a)	22.	(a)	30.	(b)	38.	(c)
7.	(b)	15.	(c)	23.	(a)	31.	(b)	39.	(b)
8.	(b)	16.	(b)	24.	(b)	32.	(a)	40.	(b)

1. (b) Denominator $= \dfrac{3}{5} \times 15 = 9$

Numerator $= \dfrac{2}{4} \times 16 = 8$

Fraction $= \dfrac{8}{9}$

2. (a) Prime number has only two factors 1 and the number itself.

3. (c) $6x = 1 \times 2 \times 3 \times 4 \times 5 \times 6 = 720$

4. (a) A number is divisible by 2 if it has at its once place 0, 2, 4, 6 or 8.
So, we add 1 to 4321 to get 4322, which is divisible by 2.

5. (c) $987.564 = 9 \times 100 + 8 \times 10 + 7 + \dfrac{5}{10} + \dfrac{6}{100} + \dfrac{4}{1000}$

6. (a) 27.027 is smallest among all.

Hints & Explanations

7. **(b)** L.C.M. of 2, 5, 4, 7

    $\begin{array}{c|cccc} 2 & 2, 5, 4, 7 \\ \hline & 1, 5, 2, 7 \end{array}$

    $= 2 \times 5 \times 2 \times 7 = 140$

    $\dfrac{1 \times 70}{2 \times 70} = \dfrac{70}{140}; \dfrac{2 \times 28}{5 \times 28} = \dfrac{56}{140}$

    $\dfrac{3 \times 35}{4 \times 35} = \dfrac{105}{140}; \dfrac{4 \times 20}{7 \times 20} = \dfrac{80}{140}$

    $\dfrac{2}{5} < \dfrac{1}{2} < \dfrac{4}{7} < \dfrac{3}{4}$

8. **(a)** $4\dfrac{3}{11} = \dfrac{47}{11}$

9. **(d)** $55 \div 11 \times 17 - 78 + 32$

    $= 5 \times 17 - 78 + 32$

    $= 85 - 78 + 32$

    $= 117 - 78 = 39$

    $39 = XXXIX$

10. **(c)** $0.6 + 7.09 - 3.002$

    $= 7.69 - 3.002$

    $= 4.688$

11. **(b)** V.U.S Laxman

12. **(c)** Total balls = (119 + 133 + 33 + 10) = 295

13. **(b)** There are 30 tens in 3 hundreds.

14. **(b)** Cost of 1 packet of TIGER biscuit = ₹ 5

    In ₹ 30, number of packets = $\dfrac{30}{5}$

    = 6

    For every two packet 1, packet biscuit is free then for 6 packet we get 3 packets free

    Total packets = 6 + 3 = 9

15. **(c)** F × B = 9 × 3 = 27

    (C × D) + B = (4 × 6) + 3 = 27

16. **(b)** Co-prime

17. **(d)** 2 × 4 × 6 × 8 = 384

18. **(d)** Sum of all angles of a quadrilateral is 360°

19. **(b)** (A) → 3, (B) → 1, (C) → 2, (D) → 4

20. **(b)**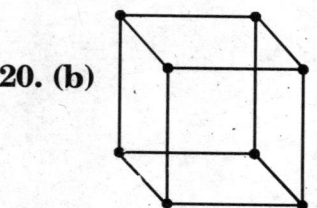

21. **(c)** 22222 − 2222 + 222 − 22 + 2

    = 20000 + 200 + 2

    = 20202

22. **(b)**

23. **(c)** $\dfrac{2}{3} = \dfrac{2 \times 4}{3 \times 4} = \dfrac{8}{12}$,

    $\dfrac{2 \times 3}{3 \times 3} = \dfrac{6}{9}, \dfrac{2 \times 2}{3 \times 2} = \dfrac{4}{6}$

24. **(b)** 20356

25. **(c)** Wire needed = Perimeter of playground

    Perimeter of playground = 2(250 + 20) = 540 m

26. **(c)** Total distance Priya has to cover to reach her daughter

    = 69 km + 389 km 540 m

    = 458 km 540 m

    Distance between Priya's home and New York

    = 345 km 255 m

Hints & Explanations

Extra distance
= 458 km 540 m − 345 km 255 m
= 113 km 285 m

27. (c) R, P, S, Q

28. (b) Capacity of tank = (8 × 380 + 1250) mL
= (3040 + 1250) mL = 4290 mL

29. (b)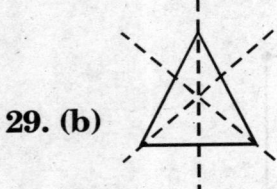

30. (d) Total days after Sunday = 7 + 5 = 12
7 days = 1 week,

31. (c) Difference in time,
1 : 30 − 1 : 20 = 10 minutes
10 × 60 = 600 seconds

32. (b) 1 week = 7 days
Number of weeks = $\frac{147}{7}$ = 21

33. (b) 2003 is not a leap year.
Therefore, February 2003 had 28 days.

34. (a) A quarter past one in the afternoon

35. (c) Ravi has 30 toy cars.
Bijji has 15 toy cars
30 = 2 × 15

36. (c) (6 #) × (4*)
= (6 + 5 + 4 + 3 + 2 + 1)
× (4 − 3)
= 21 × (1) = 21

37. (c) Cost of 24 tickets = ₹1000 × 3
= ₹3000

38. (c) 11 × 10 = 110; 4 × 5 = 20
14 × 15 = 210; 19 × 13 = 247

39. (b) XXIX = 29
XXXI = 31
29 × 31 = 899

40. (b) B : A number having only 2 factors (i.e. 1 and the number itself) is a prime number.
C : Two numbers added in any order gives same sum.

SCIENCE

MOCK TEST-1

ANSWERS KEY

1.	(d)	9.	(d)	17.	(d)	25.	(c)	33.	(c)
2.	(d)	10.	(c)	18.	(d)	26.	(b)	34.	(d)
3.	(b)	11.	(b)	19.	(a)	27.	(d)	35.	(a)
4.	(a)	12.	(b)	20.	(b)	28.	(b)	36.	(c)
5.	(d)	13.	(c)	21.	(d)	29.	(d)	37.	(c)
6.	(b)	14.	(b)	22.	(b)	30.	(b)	38.	(a)
7.	(d)	15.	(d)	23.	(d)	31.	(d)	39.	(c)
8.	(d)	16.	(c)	24.	(c)	32.	(d)	40.	(c)

1. **(d)** Reproduction and respiration of gases are the most important characteristic features of living organisms.

2. **(d)** Bacteria is considered as living. Virus becomes alive only when they are present inside a living host.

3. **(b)** Ginger — modified stem
   Radish — modified root
   Spinach — leaf is edible
   Rice — seed is the edible part

4. **(a)** During photosynthesis plants use carbon dioxide and water in presence of sunlight to produce glucose and oxygen.

5. **(d)** Leech is an ectoparasite.

6. **(b)**
   Animals   **Young ones**
   A. Butterfly   Larva
   B. Frog   Tadpole
   C. Fish   Fry
   D. Cockroach   Nymph

7. **(d)** The life cycle of a butterfly involves different stages in the order: Eggs → Caterpillar → Pupa and then finally into adult butterfly.

8. **(d)** In the respiratory system, oxygen follows the following path: Nose → Wind pipe → Lungs → Blood.

9. **(d)** P-Heart, Q-Kidney, R-Lungs, S-Stomach

10. **(c)** Our body shows reflex action, in which our body reacts spontaneously to sudden changes like heat and cold.

Hints & Explanations

11. **(b)** Vitamins are needed in small quantities for the maintainance of vital biochemical reactions in the body.
12. **(b)** In the small intestine, digestion takes place by the release of juices.
13. **(c)** Glucose gives instant energy. That is why, athletes take glucose just before the race begin.
14. **(b)** Carnivores have well - developed canines which help in crushing and tearing the food.
15. **(d)** The figure shows a molar tooth.
16. **(c)** Increase in the level of CO_2 causes global warming.
17. **(d)** Recycling can save natural resources, control pollution and can make useful things from waste materials.
18. **(d)** Organic matter cannot be recycled.
19. **(a)** Igloos are found in very cold places as they are made up of ice blocks.
20. **(b)** The windows should be in opposite direction to the door in order to facilitate cross ventilation.
21. **(d)** All of the given statements are correct.
22. **(b)** The weather remains constant throughout the year, near coastal regions.
23. **(d)** Deforestation will cause soil erosion, depletion of water catchment areas and global warming.
24. **(c)** Most of the metals are found deep inside the earth.
25. **(c)** The balloon shown in the figure (c) will be easiest to prick as it is the most inflated and stretched one.
26. **(b)** Steam converts into water upon cooling and on further cooling, converts into ice.
27. **(d)** Frictional force is responsible for stopping a moving body.
28. **(b)** The boy is applying force in pushing the table.
29. **(d)** The instrument that should be used to measure the temperature of a glass of milk is thermometer.
30. **(b)** Alpha Centauri is 4.3 light year away from Earth.
31. **(d)** Microwave oven is not used in communication. It is an appliance used for cooking food.
32. **(d)** The development of technology has resulted in increased atmospheric pollutions.

Hints & Explanations

33. (c) Smoke signal is one of the oldest forms of long distance communication. This was followed by telegraph. Telephone is the most recent among the three.

34. (d) Moon takes 27.5 days to complete one revolution around the earth.

35. (a) Mercury is very close to the Sun. This is why, it can be seen in the morning and evening.

36. (c) Fish breathe through gills. Tadpole, which develop to adult frog also respires through gills although the adult frogs have developed lungs.

37. (c) An animal that hunts for its food is called a predator.

38. (a) Telecommunication is the exchange of information between two entities by the use of technology. Nowadays we use internet to send messages and communicate with others.

39. (c) Kidneys are responsible for eliminating liquid wastes. Lungs eliminate gaseous waste. Small intestine is responsible for absorption of digested food and heart is responsible for circulation of blood.

40. (c) At the age of 5 years, 90% of weight of brain is achieved.

MOCK TEST-2
ANSWERS KEY

1.	(d)	9.	(c)	17.	(b)	25.	(c)	33.	(c)
2.	(a)	10.	(d)	18.	(d)	26.	(d)	34.	(c)
3.	(b)	11.	(d)	19.	(d)	27.	(b)	35.	(b)
4.	(a)	12.	(d)	20.	(a)	28.	(d)	36.	(d)
5.	(c)	13.	(d)	21.	(b)	29.	(b)	37.	(c)
6.	(b)	14.	(c)	22.	(c)	30.	(c)	38.	(c)
7.	(c)	15.	(d)	23.	(d)	31.	(a)	39.	(b)
8.	(d)	16.	(b)	24.	(d)	32.	(c)	40.	(a)

1. (d) Living things need air (oxygen), they grow, reproduce and respond to their environment.

2. (a) When we plant rocks and seeds, only the seeds grow and gave rise to a new plant.

Hints & Explanations

Whereas the rocks remained the same because rocks are non-living.
3. **(b)** Electrical energy
4. **(a)** Pigeons make their own nests. Cuckoos lay their eggs in the nest of other birds. Lion and tiger live in a den or a cave or in a dense forest. But they don't build their homes.
5. **(c)** In radish, food is stored in roots. Hence, the edible part of radish are their roots.
6. **(b)** Cactus plants live in desert where there is water scarcity. Thus to prevent water loss they do not have leaves. Stem becomes green to perform photosynthesis. This is called adaptation. Plants modify according to the habitat in which they live.
7. **(c)** The eggs of fish are called spawns.
8. **(d)** Snakes, birds and frogs lay eggs, whereas cats give birth to young ones.
9. **(c)** Camouflage
10. **(a)** The amount of nutrients in soil is known as soil fertility.
11. **(d)** Nervous system is responsible for controlling all the activities in human body.
12. **(d)** Urine is stored in the urinary bladder (S) temporarily from where it is released out from time to time.
13. **(d)** Pulses (gram, pea, mung, etc.) and meat are good sources of protein.
14. **(c)** Vitamin D can be synthesized in our body in the presence of sunlight.
15. **(d)** Evaporation is quickest in hot and dry weather. Humidity will slower the rate of evaporation.
16. **(b)** The teeth that are used for cracking hard food are premolars.
17. **(b)** The teeth marked 'X' are called premolars.
18. **(d)** Dams are man-made sources of water.
19. **(d)** Diarrhoea is caused due to unhygienic surroundings and bad food habits.
20. **(a)** Germs present in drinking water can be killed by boiling.
21. **(b)** Banana peels make the beach unhygienic and dirty. We should avoid littering.
22. **(c)** Houses have sloping roofs in the areas of high rain and snow fall.

Hints & Explanations

23. **(d)** Straw is used to make a kuccha house. Rest all, cement, brick and iron are used in making a pucca house.
24. **(d)** This type of change is both chemical change and physical change.
25. **(c)** The water droplets seen on grass in the winter mornings are due to condensation of water vapour present in the air.
26. **(d)** Burning of wood, respiration and flying of aeroplane, all require presence of air.
27. **(b)** Animal dung and rotten vegetables are both a very good source of manure.
28. **(d)** Garden soil contains humus, holds enough water and contain air. Hence, it is most suitable for plant growth.
29. **(b)** Conversion of solid into liquid is known as melting.
30. **(c)** Air currents are not caused due to condensation. Rest all are caused due to condensation.
31. **(a)** For a given volume, solid will have the maximum number of molelcules.
32. **(c)** A moving body stops due to applied force.
33. **(c)** A standard scale can measure minimum 1 millimeter with accuracy.
34. **(c)** To measure a curved wire, first a thread is used and then the length of the thread is measured with the help of a ruler.
35. **(b)** Ruler will be too small. Measuring cylinder is used to measure liquid. So measuring tape is the correct option.
36. **(d)** Earth, Moon and Jupiter are parts of solar system.
37. **(c)** Moon is the smallest and Sun is the largest.
38. **(c)** Cactus and camel are both adapted for a xerophytic habitat such as a desert.
39. **(b)** A – Liver – Secrete bile juice
    B – Stomach – Churning of food takes place
    C – Small intestine – Absorption of food takes place
    D – Mouth – Saliva mixes with food
40. **(d)** A. Kidney – 3. Nitrogenous waste
    B. Brain – 1. Control and coordination
    C. Tongue – 4. Taste buds
    D. Ear – 2. Sense of hearing

Hints & Explanations

MOCK TEST-3

ANSWERS KEY

1.	(a)	8.	(a)	15.	(c)	22.	(a)	29.	(a)
2.	(d)	9.	(c)	16.	(a)	23.	(a)	30.	(c)
3.	(d)	10.	(c)	17.	(b)	24.	(a)	31.	(d)
4.	(a)	11.	(a)	18.	(b)	25.	(b)	32.	(b)
5.	(c)	12.	(a)	19.	(d)	26.	(b)	33.	(d)
6.	(d)	13.	(b)	20.	(c)	27.	(b)	34.	(c)
7.	(a)	14.	(b)	21.	(b)	28.	(b)	35.	(b)

1. **(a)** Pathogen is the microorganism which cause diseases.
2. **(d)** Canine teeth and strong claws help the carnivorous animals to catch and kill their prey and to chew the flesh.
3. **(d)** The biggest natural satelllite of the planet Saturn is 'Titan'.
4. **(a)** Elephant is a mammal.
5. **(c)** Earth attracts Moon with gravitational force.
6. **(d)** Petroleum is the fossil fuel.
7. **(a)** When the incoming light is sent back after hitting an object, the phenomena is called reflection of light.
8. **(a)** The given figure shows a spiral galaxy.
9. **(c)** Oxygen is essential for the process of burning.
10. **(c)** Sublimation is the process of conversion of solid directly into gas without going into liquid state.
11. **(a)** Pressure is defined as force applied per unit area. Thus greater surface area means less pressure.
12. **(a)** Bus
13. **(b)** Ozone is found in the stratosphere.
14. **(b)** Enamel
15. **(c)** Intermolecular force is minimum in gases and maximum in solid.
16. **(a)** The bubbles are formed when the gases dissolved in water get separated on heating.
17. **(b)** On heating the substance, the force between the molecules gets weakened and the molecules start moving apart.
18. **(b)** Jupiter is the largest planet, Saturn being the second largest.
19. **(d)** Wood, dead plants and animals all are biodegradable.
20. **(c)**

Dog is a carnivorous animal rest others are herbivorous animals.
21. **(b)** Souring of milk is a chemical change.

Hints & Explanations

22. **(a)** Slate is a metamorphic rock.
23. **(a)** Kinetic energy is directly proportional to the speed. Hence, the object moving with greater speed will possess higher amount of kinetic energy.
24. **(a)** The figure shows air pollution caused by smoke released from factories. It is polluting the environment, therefore it is not good.
25. **(b)** Change of shape is a physical change as the properties of the new object (plastic bottle) remain the same.
26. **(b)** Microorganisms are biotic, rest all are abiotic.
27. **(b)** Since the ball is in motion it has kinetic energy.
28. **(b)** Water pollution
29. **(a)** Sense of smell and taste are linked.
30. **(c)** Stretched rubber band has tension force.
31. **(d)** Soil is formed by weathering of rocks.
32. **(b)** Gravitational force is a weak force which acts between any two pieces of matter in the universe.
33. **(d)** Urea, water and salts are removed by kidney.
34. **(c)** Gliding joint is responsible for sideways movement.
35. **(b)** Water exists in all three states. Change of ice into water is a physical change. Atom is the basic unit of matter. Molecules are the smallest particles that exist independently.

MOCK TEST-4

ANSWERS KEY

1	(b)	8	(c)	15	(d)	22	(a)	29	(d)
2	(a)	9	(a)	16	(d)	23	(d)	30	(c)
3	(d)	10	(b)	17	(d)	24	(c)	31	(a)
4	(b)	11	(c)	18	(a)	25	(c)	32	(a)
5	(b)	12	(c)	19	(a)	26	(b)	33	(a)
6	(c)	13	(a)	20	(d)	27	(b)	34	(a)
7	(b)	14	(a)	21	(b)	28	(d)	35	(d)

1. **(b)** Brain is protected by a hard bony structure called skull.
2. **(a)** Potential energy increases with increase in height.
3. **(d)** This is both physical change and chemical change because the properties of water are different from properties of hydrogen and oxygen.
4. **(b)** Aman is right, Rahul is wrong because biodegradable substances do not cause pollution.

Hints & Explanations

5. **(b)** Animals go for winter sleep so as to avoid extreme cold conditions and scarcity of food.

6. **(c)** Porcupine is also known as "Touch-me-not" animal. They puff their spine, when in danger and become difficult to touch.

7. **(b)** The correct sequence of changes in a butterfly are – Egg – caterpillar – pupa – adult butterfly.

8. **(c)** An object floats in water due to upthrust force.

9. **(a)** The meteors burn due to friction.

10. **(b)** 'g' is gravitational acceleration.

11. **(c)** Asteroids occur between orbits of Mars and Jupiter.

12. **(c)** Nervous system transfers information from brain to different parts of body.

13. **(a)** Humus helps in the growth of plant.

14. **(a)** Terrace farming helps in reducing soil erosion. Terrace farming uses steps that are built into the side of a mountain. On each level, various crops are planted. When it rains, instead of wasting away all the nutrients in the soil, the nutrients are carried down to the next level.

15. **(d)** Malaria is caused by plasmodium parasite which is a protozoa.

16. **(d)** Burning of candle is both physical and chemical change. Burning of candle melts the wax, and hence, physical state of wax had changed from solid to liquid. (This is a physical change).
Wax combines with the atmospheric oxygen and changes to carbon dioxide, heat and light. (This is a chemical change).

17. **(d)** Kidney is responsible for filtering water from blood.

18. **(a)** When clothes dry in air, water present in the clothes get converted into water vapour. This process is known as evaporation.

19. **(a)** The given substance is in solid state. The spaces between the molecules are very less in solid.

20. **(d)** Earthworm is an invertebrate.

21. **(b)** Waxy coating present on the surface of the leaves of aquatic plants are to prevent rotting.

22. **(a)** The gliding joint allows movement of the wrist and ankle.

23. **(d)** Food rich in vitamin and mineral give us strength to flight against diseases.

24. **(c)** Frictional force works only when objects are in contact with each other.

Hints & Explanations

25. **(c)** In the world, Tamil Nadu holds the 2nd position in the use of wind energy to produce electricity.
26. **(b)** Photosynthesis produces glucose.
27. **(b)** The food we eat, is digested and ultimately energy is released through a series of chemical reaction. Hence, it is a chemical change.
28. **(d)** Kidney is involved in excretion and has no role in digestion.
29. **(d)** Fossil fuels are non-renewable, rest all are renewable.
30. **(c)** The characteristics of leaves mentioned here are possessed by aquatic plants (that grow in water).
31. **(a)** Potential energy of an object is due to its position while kinetic energy is due to its motion.
32. **(a)** Sweetened condensed milk is rich in calories.
33. **(a)** The earth rotates from West to East.
34. **(a)** The stationary stone (which is not in motions) has potential energy.

35. **(d)** A. Heart — 4. is a hollow, muscular organ
    B. Stomach — 3. digests food
    C. Intestine — 1. is located between the stomach and the anus.
    D. Lungs — 2. are paired organs

MOCK TEST-5

ANSWERS KEY

1	(b)	8	(a)	15	(a)	22	(b)	29	(b)
2	(c)	9	(b)	16	(c)	23	(d)	30	(c)
3	(c)	10	(b)	17	(b)	24	(c)	31	(a)
4	(c)	11	(a)	18	(d)	25	(b)	32	(a)
5	(c)	12	(d)	19	(a)	26	(b)	33	(a)
6	(a)	13	(a)	20	(c)	27	(d)	34	(a)
7	(c)	14	(c)	21	(c)	28	(c)	35	(c)

1. **(b)** Aeroplanes travel at a supersonic speed.
2. **(c)** Air pressure is the pressure exerted by the air in the atmosphere.
3. **(c)** Kinetic energy of an object is the energy that it possessed due to its motion.
4. **(c)** Force is the push or pull of an object.
5. **(c)** Photosynthesis is the process used by green plants to prepare food in the presence of sunlight.
6. **(a)** Sensory nerves carries the messages from the sense organs to the spinal cord or brain.

Hints & Explanations

7. **(c)** Rubber, glass, plastic are good insulators which do not allow heat to pass through them.
8. **(a)** 'Y' represents hen. Hen is a bird which lays egg and breathes with the help of lungs.
9. **(b)** 'S' represents evaporation in which water changes into water vapour.
10. **(b)** Ice is solid. The forces of attraction is highest in solid.
11. **(a)** Houses in hot and dry regions have thick flat roofs as these houses are warmer in winter and cooler in summer.
12. **(d)** Vitamins and minerals are protective nutrients.
13. **(a)** The direction of ball will be changed due to the application of force.
14. **(c)** Talcum powder is sprinkled on the carrom board to reduce friction force so that the carrom coins can move faster on the carrom board.
15. **(a)** The time taken by the earth to move around the sun is 1 year (365 days).
16. **(c)** A force that pulls the object together is called force of attraction.
17. **(b)** Players give kinetic energy during striking the ball with cue stick.
18. **(d)** The tiny part of a seed that grows into a plant is known as embryo.
19. **(a)** Solid has definite shape and volume.
20. **(c)** When a cup of water (which is a liquid) is put into a freezer it will form ice (which is a solid).
21. **(c)** Erosion is the process in which rock material is being moved over Earth surface by wind and water.
22. **(b)** In order to maintain good health, humans should exercise regularly.
23. **(d)** The fins of a fish helps the fish to move in water.
24. **(c)** All living things need nutrients and have the capacity to grow.
25. **(b)** This process represents life cycle in which seed get converted into a mature tree which produce more seeds.
26. **(b)** A group of camel is known as flock.
27. **(d)** Cows have external ears.
28. **(c)** The roots that are present above the ground are called aerial roots.
29. **(b)** Ivy is not an edible flower.
30. **(c)** Aquatic animals live in water.
31. **(a)** Water pollution occurs when pollutants are discharged directly or indirectly into water bodies.
32. **(a)** Evaporation of water in test-tube will be slowest because the surface area of the mouth of the test-tube is very less as compared to others.
33. **(a)** Crop rotation is used to retain the quality of soil and its mineral content.
34. **(a)** Condensation is the process of changing the water vapour (gas) into water (liquid).
35. **(c)** The largest river of India is Ganga.

GENERAL KNOWLEDGE

MOCK TEST 1

ANSWER KEY

1.	(b)	6.	(d)	11.	(c)	16.	(a)	21.	(c)
2.	(d)	7.	(d)	12.	(a)	17.	(b)	22.	(d)
3.	(b)	8.	(c)	13.	(a)	18.	(b)	23.	(d)
4.	(a)	9.	(a)	14.	(a)	19.	(c)	24.	(a)
5.	(b)	10.	(a)	15.	(b)	20.	(d)	25.	(b)

1. **(b)** Larynx is located between the pharynx and the trachea and contains the vocal cords which produce sound.
2. **(d)** Cow eats only plants, so it is a herbivore.
3. **(b)** Vladimir Putin is the President of Russia.
4. **(a)** Stomata help in respiration and transpiration of plants through which exchange of carbon dioxide, oxygen and water vapour take place.
5. **(b)** Yeast is a category of fungi which is added while making bread.
6. **(d)** Carbon dioxide is also called a greenhouse gas as it causes global warming. It is also used by plants along with water to carry out photosynthesis.
7. **(d)** Human beings belong to the class of mammals as they give birth to young ones and are warm-blooded. Amphibians live in both land and water and lay eggs. Birds have feathers and also lay eggs. Reptiles are cold-blooded and also lay eggs.
8. **(c)** The Din-e-Ilahi or "Religion of God" was started by the Mughal emperor Akbar the Great in 1582 AD, to have the best quality of all the religions of his empire.
9. **(a)** The song was adopted in its Hindi version by the Constituent Assembly of India as the National Anthem on 24 January 1950.
10. **(a)** There are 24 spokes in Ashok chakra of our national flag which signifies *dharma*.
11. **(c)** Hans Lippershey is known for the earliest written record of a refracting telescope.
12. **(a)** Saturn is the sixth planet in the Solar system and, when seen through a telescope, appears as the most beautiful planet. Earth has one large natural satellite, known as the Moon.
13. **(a)** Water is released in the atmosphere through evaporation and by plants. Water vapor then forms cloud which then condenses back to water. Water then fall on the Earth in the form of rainfall.
14. **(a)** Acid rain is caused due to presence of some gases like carbon dioxide in the rain water. Acid rain causes damage to buildings.
15. **(b)** The first European to document the area was a French priest, Father Louis Hennepin. During a 1678 expedition, he was overwhelmed by the size and

Hints & Explanations

16. (a) PhD stands for Doctor of Philosophy, which is a type of doctoral degree awarded by universities in many countries

17. (b) Kaa is a fictional character from 'The Jungle Book' stories and is one of Mowgli's mentors and friends.

18. (b) Kathakali dance form is inspired by folk arts and involves music, vocal performers, choreography and hand and facial gestures.

19. (c) Paragliding is the recreational sport of flying paragliders.

20. (d) Viswanathan Anand is an Indian chess player Grandmaster and a former World Chess Champion. He became India's first grandmaster in 1988.

significance of Niagara Falls. When he returned to France, Hennepin published an account of his travels in "A New Discovery." The book brought Niagara Falls to the attention of the western world for the first time and inspired further exploration of the region.

21. (c) The given pictogram depicts the game of wrestling.

22. (d) The given sign shows that no parking is allowed in a given area.

23. (d) Droupadi Murmu was born to a Santali family on 20 June 1958, in Uparbeda village in the Baidaposi area of Rairangpur, Odisha. Her father Biranchi Narayan Tudu was a farmer. She is an Indian politician who is serving as the 15th and current President of India since 2022. She is the first person belonging to the tribal community. She has also served as the governor of Jharkhand from the year 2015 to 2021. She has also previously served as a member of the Legislative Assembly from Odisha and minister of state of the Government of Odisha.

24. (a)

25. (b) Sir Edward Lutyens was an British architect. He designed many buildings in India including India Gate, and he also designed viceroy's house which is known as the Rashtrapati Bhavan.

MOCK TEST 2

ANSWER KEY

1.	(b)	6.	(d)	11.	(d)	16.	(d)	21.	(a)
2.	(c)	7.	(c)	12.	(c)	17.	(d)	22.	(b)
3.	(a)	8.	(b)	13.	(b)	18.	(a)	23.	(c)
4.	(c)	9.	(a)	14.	(b)	19.	(c)	24.	(a)
5.	(d)	10.	(d)	15.	(b)	20.	(a)	25.	(b)

1. (b) Lower chambers of the heart are called ventricles & the upper chambers are called auricles.

2. (c) Neuron is a part of central nervous system.

3. (a) Lacrimal glands are paired, almond-shaped glands in our eyes which produce clear liquid called tear.

4. (c) Petunia is a flowering plant of South American origin. Yeast is a fungi. Bacteria is a microarganism and lichen is a combination of fungi and bacteria.

Hints & Explanations

5. **(d)** Cactus is a plant which is adapted to grow in desert as its leaves is suited to grow in dry area.
6. **(d)** Bacteria and Fungi decompose the dead organic matters and help in recycling them in the environment.
7. **(c)** Camouflage is the ability of animals to take the appearance of the environment for their protection.
8. **(b)** France is the currency of Switzerland. Krone, Dollar and Ringgit are the currencies of Norway, United States, and Malaysia, respectively.
9. **(a)** Lord Buddha, also known as Gautam Buddha, was born in Lumbini, now in modern-day Nepal, and raised in the Shakya capital of Kapilvastu.
10. **(d)** The crimson red national flag of Nepal is a simplified combination of two single triangular tailed figures.
11. **(d)** Eratosthenes of Cyrene is best known for being the first person to calculate the circumference of the Earth.
12. **(c)** Dynamo is a device which produces electricity by being rotated by the fall of water or by other source.
13. **(b)** When a volcano erupts, hot molten liquid comes out through an opening. This liquid is called lava.
14. **(b)** The Kinetoscope is an early motion picture exhibition device, designed for films to be viewed by one person at a time through a peephole viewer window. Most of this invention work was performed by Edison's assistant, William Kennedy Laurie Dickson, beginning in 1888.
15. **(b)** Lichens are useful bio-indicators for air pollution, especially sulfur dioxide pollution, since they get their water & essential nutrients mainly from the atmosphere rather than from the soil.
16. **(d)** Regular servicing of the car will prevent the emission of smoke causing air pollution.
17. **(d)** CNG or compressed natural gas is actually the cleanest of all fossil fuels. It is composed mainly of methane, which burns to produce carbon dioxide and water vapor.
18. **(a)** Greta Tintin Eleonora Ernman Thunberg was born on 3 January 2003, in Stockholm, Sweden, the daughter of opera singer Malena Ernman and actor Svante Thunberg. Her paternal grandfather was actor & director Olof Thunberg. Thunberg's activism began when she persuaded her parents to adopt lifestyle choices that reduced their own carbon footprint. In August 2018, at age 15, she started spending her Fridays outside the Swedish Parliament to call for stronger action on climate change.
19. **(c)** Jnanpith Award, a research and cultural institute founded in 1944 by industrialist Sahu Shanti Prasad Jain of the Sahu Jain family, conceived an idea in May 1961 to start a scheme commanding national prestige and of international standard to select the best book out of the publications in Indian languages.
20. **(a)** The first Olympic games was held in 1896 in Athens, Greece.
21. **(a)** Sachin Tendulkar has scored over 10,000 runs in one-day international cricket.
22. **(b)** Kyaiktiyo Pagoda is one of the world's most important pilgrim

sites to Buddhists and the second most important in all of Myanmar. It's known around the world and people flock there from far and wide to experience it in person. The Golden Rock that's placed on the edge of a hill is of great importance.

23. **(c)** Dr. S. Jaishankar, External Affairs Minister held the inauguration ceremony of the Buzi Bridge. It is indigenously built in Mozambique as part of the 132 km Tika-Buji-Nova-Sofala road project. Dr. S. Jaishankar visited for a meeting with the Speaker of the Assembly Esperanca Bias in Maputo, Mozambique. Mozambique is a Southern African country with popular beaches and marine parks. The capital is Maputo whereas its currency is the Mozambican medical.

24. **(a)** The tiger population by the year 2022 has significantly escalated to 3167 which is nearly 200 more than the last year's data. The number of tigers in India was 1,411 in 2006 which rose to 1,706 by 2010. This number had increased to 2,226 by 2014. PM Modi went to Mysore in Karnataka on the occasion of completing 50 years of 'Project Tiger' and also visited Bandipur Tiger Reserve.

25. **(b)** Delhi Capitals captain David Warner creates history by becoming the fastest batsman to score 6000 runs in the Indian Premier League (IPL-2023). This happened while playing a match against Rajasthan Royals held at the Barsapara Stadium in Guwahati. after Royal Challengers Bangalore's Virat Kohli and Punjab Kings captain Shikhar Dhawan, he is now the only third batsman to join this prestigious group. David Warner has attained this feat in 165 innings.

MOCK TEST 3

ANSWER KEY

1.	(d)	6.	(a)	11.	(b)	16.	(b)	21.	(a)
2.	(c)	7.	(d)	12.	(a)	17.	(a)	22.	(a)
3.	(c)	8.	(a)	13.	(c)	18.	(a)	23.	(a)
4.	(d)	9.	(a)	14.	(c)	19.	(b)	24.	(a)
5.	(d)	10.	(d)	15.	(d)	20.	(b)	25.	(d)

1. **(d)** Canines are sharp, pointed teeth, which help tear food.
2. **(c)** Blood oxygenation takes place in the lungs, and the liver helps in food digestion.
3. **(c)** Egg is rich in protein and should be consumed regularly to get enough protein.
4. **(d)** Stapes is the smallest bone in our body. It is located in the inner year.
5. **(d)** Water, carbon dioxide, and light are required by plants to prepare food by the process of photosynthsis. Oxygen is not needed to prepare food.

Hints & Explanations

6. **(a)** Cockroach breathes through circular openings on their skin called spiracles.
7. **(d)** Habitat is the natural habitat of animals where they interact with other animals.
8. **(a)** Ginger is a modified stem, whereas radish, carrot and beetroot are examples of root modification.
9. **(a)** The people of Tibet are called Tibetans.
10. **(d)** Whooper swan is the national bird of Finland.
11. **(b)** Alpha Centauri is the closest star system to the Solar System and is 4.37 light-years away from the Sun.
12. **(a)** Iron is a magnetic substance which is attracted by a magnet.
13. **(c)** Use of fertilizers in fields cause water pollution. Carbon dioxide is a greenhouse gas which causes heating of the Earth.
14. **(c)** Soil pollution causes loss in soil fertility resulting into barren land. Minamata is caused due to pollution of water with mercury. Lung disease is caused due to air pollution.
15. **(d)** Both bio-fertilizer and crop rotation help in increasing soil fertility without causing environmental pollution.
16. **(b)** The 10th edition of the annual bilateral maritime exercise SLINEX-2023 are to be hosted jointly by the Indian Navy & Sri Lanka Navy at Colombo starting April 03, 2023, up to April 08. The Indian Navy is represented by INS Kiltan and INS Savitri whereas the Sri Lankan Navy is represented by SLNS Vijayabahu and SLNS Samudura.
17. **(a)** Kalidas is also known as the 'Shakespeare of India'.
18. **(a)** European nation Finland is now the 31st member of the military alliance NATO. It was necessary as Finland is a neighbouring country of Russia and shares a border of nearly 1300 kilometres with Russia. Both Finland and Sweden applied for NATO membership after Russia assailed Ukraine in 2022.
19. **(b)** Amjad Ali Khan is a famous Indian sarod player.
20. **(b)** Football is the national game of Italy.
21. **(b)** Niraj Nigam is the new Executive Director at the Reserve Bank of India (RBI) with effect from April 03. Previously, he was the Director of the Regional Office of RBI in Bhopal. He will now take charge of four departments including consumer education and protection as part of his new job.
22. **(a)** African country Kenya is recently going to launch its first operational Earth observation satellite named 'Taifa-1' by April 11, 2023. The Kenya Space Agency will blast this spacecraft with a SpaceX Falcon 9 rocket from the Vandenberg Space Force Base in California.
23. **(a)** Bangladesh all-rounder Shakib Al Hasan has become the highest wicket-taker in the T20I format. Shakib Al Hasan has now registered 136 wickets. Shakib achieved this feat against Ireland. In terms of most wickets, he has left behind Tim Southee of New Zealand who has 134 wickets in his name.
24. **(a)** India's first multi-sports museum has been opened in Kolkata.
25. **(d)** Highest Civilian Award of Assam for the year 2023 'Assam Baibhav' Awarded to renowned medical practitioner Dr Tapan Saikia. He has been given

this award for his remarkable contribution to the field of healthcare (cancer care) and public service. He has been given this honour by the Governor of Assam Gulab Chand Kataria during a program organized in Guwahati.

MOCK TEST 4

ANSWER KEY

1.	(d)	9.	(c)	17.	(d)	25.	(b)	33.	(a)
2.	(c)	10.	(c)	18.	(c)	26.	(a)	34.	(c)
3.	(b)	11.	(c)	19.	(a)	27.	(a)	35.	(a)
4.	(d)	12.	(c)	20.	(c)	28.	(c)	36.	(b)
5.	(d)	13.	(d)	21.	(d)	29.	(b)	37.	(d)
6.	(b)	14.	(c)	22.	(d)	30.	(b)	38.	(a)
7.	(b)	15.	(c)	23.	(b)	31.	(c)	39.	(a)
8.	(b)	16.	(b)	24.	(c)	32.	(b)	40.	(c)

1. **(d)** Lungs are not used during digestion. They are used for the exchange of gases in blood.

2. **(c)** Salad is a good source of fibre. Meat is rich in fat and protein.

3. **(b)** Urine formation takes place in Kidney. Harmful substances from the body and excess water are removed in kidney in the form of urine.

4. **(d)** Vitreous humour is the clear gel that fills the space between the lens and the retina. Aqueous humour is a transparent, watery fluid which fills the front chamber of the eye.

5. **(d)** Functions of roots are to absorb water from soil, absorb nutrients from soil, and fix the plant to the soil.

6. **(b)** Hibernation is a state of inactivity in an organism that maintains its body at a metabolically favourable temperature.

7. **(b)** Plants respire through stomata. Lungs, gills, and skin are the respiratory organs in humans, fish, and earthworms, respectively.

8. **(b)** Leaf is modified into a structure that traps insects.

9. **(c)** Mohiniyattam is the classical dance form from Kerala.

10. **(c)** Ellora is one of the largest rock-cut monastery-temple caves complexes in the world, and a UNESCO World Heritage Site in Maharashtra, India.

11. **(c)** Sunita Williams remained in space for 195 days during her first space flight.

12. **(c)** Archimedes, a Greek mathematician, physicist, engineer, inventor, and astronomer, gave the laws of floating bodies for the first time.

13. **(d)** Both Plastic toys and credit card are non-biodegradable because

Hints & Explanations

they are made up of plastic, which cannot be decomposed by microorganisms.

14. (c) A wind turbine is a source of green energy because wind energy does not cause pollution and are available in abundant amount.

15. (c) The ingredients of the brownies were stirred first and then were left for 15 minutes to get cooked. After the food was cooked, it was eaten by the boys.

16. (b) Padma Lakshmi from Kerala became the first transgender lawyer from the state to enrol as an advocate with the Bar Council of the state. Her goal is to ensure justice for the poor and marginalised. She was among 1,529 law graduates who were handed over Bar Enrollment Certificates at an event in Kerala.

17. (d) Recently, the World Happiness Report has been released, in which the countries of the world have been ranked on the basis of various parameters. Finland has once again emerged as the happiest country in the world. Finland has topped The World Happiness Report 2023, published by the United Nations Sustainable Development Solutions Network, for the sixth year in a row.

18. (c) The Border Roads Organisation will construct the world's highest tunnel at Shinku La Pass at 16,580 feet to connect Himachal Pradesh to Ladakh. BRO Director General Lieutenant General Rajeev Chaudhary stated this while opening the strategically important Himachal to Zanskar Road at Shinku La Pass.

19. (a) The name of the spider was Charlotte.

20. (c) The Chamera Dam is located near the town of Dalhousie, in the Chamba district of Himachal Pradesh. It impounds the River Ravi and supports the hydroelectricity project in the region. The reservoir of the dam is the Chamera Lake. The catchment of the dam is 472.5 square kilometres. The reservoir has a live storage capacity of 110 MCN and mean annual inflow of 1,273 BCM.

21. (d) Uttar Pradesh shares boundary with maximum number of other Indian states. It shares its border with Uttarakhand, Himachal Pradesh, Haryana, Rajasthan, Madhya Pradesh, Chhattisgarh, Jharkhand, Bihar as well as Delhi

22. (d) Farhan Akhtar played the role of Milkha singh in the film.

23. (b) 'Godan' has been written by Munshi Premchand. His other works include 'Rangbhoomi', 'Gaban' and 'Pratigya'.

24. (c) Down's syndrome, also known as trisomy 21, is a genetic disorder caused by the presence of all or part of a third copy of chromosome 21. Down's syndrome is the most common chromosome abnormality in humans. It is typically associated with a delay in cognitive ability (mental retardation, or MR)..

25. (b) Legendary musician and Santoor player Pandit Shivkumar Sharma passed away recently at the age of 84. He is known for popularising the santoor instrument. Pandit Shivkumar Sharma received the prestigious

Padma Shri in 1991, and the Padma Vibhushan in 2001.

26. (a) The Indian Railway Catering and Tourism Corporation (IRCTC) has announced a tour package named 'Baba Saheb Ambedkar Yatra'. This tour package covers some significant sites associated with the life of Dr. Bhim Rao Ambedkar including Dr. Ambedkar Nagar, Nagpur, Sanchi, Varanasi, Gaya, Rajgir, and Nalanda. The tour is part of the 'Dekho Apna Desh' initiative to promote domestic tourism.

27. (a) Polo is a team sport played on horseback. The objective is to score goals against an opposing team. Players score by driving a small white plastic or wooden ball into the opposing team's goal.

28. (c) They are reptiles as they have dry skin covered with scales and breathe through lungs.

29. (b) The Oil India Limited (OIL) commissioned India's first 99.999 percent pure green hydrogen plant in the state of Assam. OIL, the second largest national production and exploration firm commissioned the green hydrogen plant at its Jorhat Pump Station.

30. (b) Laika was first living organism to go to space.

31. (c) Our body contains several enzymes which help in the digestion of food. For example, enzyme pepsin is used to digest proteins.

32. (b) Skin is an organ. Alcohol consumption damages the liver. Humans cannot control heart beat. Plants require carbon dioxide to carry out photosynthesis.

33. (a) Herbs are any seed-bearing plant which does not have a woody stem and dies down to the ground after flowering.

34. (c) A camel's hump stores fat which it uses as nourishment when food is scarce.

35. (a) Typhoid is caused by bacteria Salmonella typhi. Influenza, Ring worm and Malaria are caused by virus, fungi and protozoa, respectively.

36. (b) Vitamin C is found in citrus fruits like grapes, oranges and lemon.

37. (d) The best way to preserve food is regular heating, cooling and drying. These processes do not allow growth of microorganisms which spoil our food.

38. (a) Bats produce sound to find out the location of other organisms they feed on.

39. (a) Merging with its surrounding is called camouflage.

40. (c) Carbon monoxide is a poisonous gas which can cause suffocation and even death if trapped in a closed room. It can combine with the hemoglobin of our blood.

Hints & Explanations

MOCK TEST 5

ANSWER KEY

1.	(a)	9.	(a)	17.	(c)	25.	(b)	33.	(d)
2.	(a)	10.	(c)	18.	(a)	26.	(b)	34.	(c)
3.	(d)	11.	(c)	19.	(b)	27.	(b)	35.	(d)
4.	(d)	12.	(c)	20.	(b)	28.	(b)	36.	(b)
5.	(b)	13.	(c)	21.	(b)	29.	(b)	37.	(d)
6.	(a)	14.	(a)	22.	(a)	30.	(b)	38.	(b)
7.	(a)	15.	(c)	23.	(d)	31.	(c)	39.	(c)
8.	(c)	16.	(a)	24.	(d)	32.	(c)	40.	(b)

1. (a) Trachea is a tube-like structure in the respiratory system while helps in the passage of air to and from the lung.
2. (a) Radish can be eaten as salad after washing.
3. (d) Appendix is a blind-ended tube connected to the cecum.
4. (d) Alcohol consumption damages kidneys and causes disease called liver cirrhosis.
5. (b) Adult human beings have 206 bones in their body.
6. (a) Melanin gives human skin, hair, and eyes their colour. Dark-skinned people have more melanin in their skin than light-skinned people have.
7. (a) Yeasts are single-celled micro-organisms classified as members of the fungus kingdom.
8. (c) Photosynthesis happens only in plants because it has green-coloured pigment called chlorophyll which is absent in animals. Chlorophyll is required to carry out photosynthesis.
9. (a) Petals are coloured part of a flower which helps in attracting insects for pollination. Sepals are green-coloured parts below the petals. Stamens and pistils help in reproduction. Petals protect the pitils where seeds are formed.
10. (c) Monkeys are arboreal animals because they spend the majority of their lives on trees. Aerial animals, such as birds, can naturally fly in the air. Terrestrial animals such as human beings live on land. Aquatic animals, for example fish, live in water.
11. (c) Proteins are building blocks of the body.
12. (c) Bile is produced in the liver and helps in the digestion of fats.
13. (c) Hibernation is the condition in which animals remain inactive in the winter season to escape from cold environment.
14. (a) Arunachal Pradesh has nearly 500 species of orchids.
15. (c) Manohar Parrikar, Sarbananda Sonowal, Naveen Patnaik and Pawan Kumar Chamling are the chief ministers of Goa, Assam, Odisha, and Sikkim, respectively.

Hints & Explanations

16. **(a)** Indian Museum in Kolkata is the largest museum in India.

17. **(c)** Cassini–Huygens is a spacecraft sent to the planet Saturn. Cassini is the fourth space probe to visit Saturn and the first to enter orbit.

18. **(a)** Kalpana Chawla was an astronaut from Karnal, Haryana, India, who died on February 1, 2003.

19. **(b)** The speed of light is 299792458 meter per second. Light has the maximum speed than all other objects on the Earth.

20. **(b)** Earthquakes can be detected with the help of seismograph. They are measered on Q scale called Richter scale.

21. **(b)** Oxygen is required by all living beings for respiration. It is produced by plants during photosynthesis.

22. **(a)** Trees help in preventing soil erosion by binding the soils. Coal is not a renewable resource because it gets lost after being used and cannot be recycled in nature.

23. **(d)** Terrace farming and planting trees help in preventing soil erosion. Grazing increases soil erosion.

24. **(d)** Oil spill in the ocean, burning fossil fuels, and throwing trash on the ground, cause environmental pollution.

25. **(b)** The Film Federation of India has announced the Gujarati film, Chhello Show as India's official entry to the Oscars 2023. The film, which is titled Last Film Show in English, has been selected in the Best International Feature Film category.

26. **(b)** Chief Minister Y.S Jagan Mohan Reddy paid tributes to 'People's poet' Gurram Jashuva on his 127 th birth anniversary. Jashuva used verse poetry as a weapon to wage a war against superstitions and evil of untouchability being practised in those times. He also fought against caste discrimination, poverty and economic disparities.

27. **(b)** The Union Home Ministry has facilitated the visit of Indian Sikh pilgrims to Nankana Sahib in Pakistan on the occasion of Gurupurab. A total of 2420 Indian Sikh pilgrims departed for Pakistan to participate in the Guru Nanak Jayanti celebrations with a ten-day Pakistani Pilgrim Visa. A total of 433 pilgrims from India visited Sri Kartarpur Sahib Gurdwara in Pakistan on the occasion of Gurupurab.

28. **(b)** James Cameron directed the film 'Titanic' which was released in the year 1997.

29. **(b)** Prime Minister Narendra Modi presented US president Joe Biden with a Kangra miniature painting from Himachal Pradesh on the concluding day of the 17th G20 summit in Indonesia's Bali. The Prime Minister gave Spanish Prime Minister Pedro Sanchez a Kanal brass set from Himachal's Mandi and Kullu districts and Italy's prime minister, Giorgia Meloni- a Patan Patola dupatta – handwoven from northern Gujarat.

Hints & Explanations

30. **(b)** Hornbill Festival of Nagaland, also known as the 'Festival of Festivals', showcases Nagaland's rich culture. India assumed the G20 presidency on 1st December 2022 and the 23rd Hornbill Festival 2022 also began on the same day in Nagaland. It is organized by the Government of Nagaland, to encourage inter-tribal interaction and to promote the cultural heritage of Nagaland.

31. **(c)** Andhra Pradesh Tourism Ministry re-launched the refurbished 'Bodhisiri' cruise boat operated by the state Tourism Development Corporation in Krishna River, at Punnami Ghat. The boat was originally launched by former Chief Minister the late Y. S. Rajasekhara Reddy in 2004, and it was taken off the river in 2019 due to repairs.

32. **(c)** Aerobic exercise requires pumping of oxygenated blood by the heart to deliver oxygen to working muscles. Blood pumping rate to and from the heart remain normal while talking.

33. **(d)** Odisha's Dhenkanal forest department has announced plans to install automatic sirens near its national highway to protect elephants from accidents. These sensor-based sirens will ring and a red light will turn on when elephants cross the road to alert drivers within a distance of up to 1 kilometre. The pilot project has been initiated by 'Change', a voluntary organization.

34. **(c)** Family should always make plans to escape a fire before there is a fire in our home.

35. **(d)** Cars make the street dangerous for kids. Obey all traffic signals, and if you are under age 10, ask an adult to help you cross the street.

36. **(b)** 5th June is celebrated as World Environment Day.

37. **(d)** The Defence Ministry announced that the Pune-based Defence Institute of Advanced Technology (DIAT) has developed a microwave steriliser 'Atulya' that can disintegrate the novel Coronavirus within 30 seconds by differential heating in the range of 56 degrees to 60 degrees celsius temperatures.

38. **(b)** Bile, an emulsifier liquid, is made by the liver and later stored in the gallbladder and released in the duodenum. Bile is composed of bile salts, cholesterol and bile pigments.

39. **(c)** Project Kavach is related to AIDS. The AIDS virus can be transmitted through contact with infected blood, semen or vaginal fluids. Within a few weeks of HIV infection, flu-like symptoms such as fever, sore throat and fatigue can occur.

40. **(b)** Arvind Kejriwal of Aam Aadmi Party in the current Chief Minister of Delhi.

LOGICAL REASONING

MOCK TEST-1

ANSWERS KEY

1.	(c)	7.	(c)	13.	(a)	19.	(c)	25.	(a)
2.	(c)	8.	(c)	14.	(c)	20.	(d)	26.	(a)
3.	(a)	9.	(c)	15.	(d)	21.	(a)	27.	(a)
4.	(b)	10.	(a)	16.	(b)	22.	(c)	28.	(c)
5.	(d)	11.	(c)	17.	(d)	23.	(b)	29.	(c)
6.	(a)	12.	(a)	18.	(c)	24.	(b)	30.	(d)

1. (c) Pattern followed

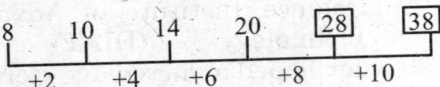

2. (c) Word formed is POLICE, i.e., arrangement of numbers should be 2, 5, 4, 1, 6, 3.

3. (a) B R A I N cannot be made from the given word.

4. (b) Colour of parrot is green and green is called red.

5. (d) %3$#

6. (a)

7. (c)

8. (c)

9. (c) Figure (X)

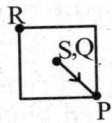

Mirror

10. (a)

Mirror

11. (c)

12. (a)

13. (a) New Positions if 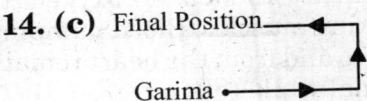, then

14. (c) Final Position

Garima

She will facing west.

15. (d)

Day before yesterday	Yesterday	Today	Tomorrow	Day after tomorrow
Friday	Saturday	Sunday	Monday	Tuesday

16. (b) Fourth Monday of January 20XX is 22nd. Hence, Rohan will celebrate his birthday on 23rd Jan.

17. (d) In left pair, second figure is the first element of first figure and becomes shaded.

Hints & Explanations

18. (c) Figures in (a), (b) and (d) are divided in eight equal parts.

19. (c) Let the number be x.
Then, x + 13x = 112
14x = 112
x = 8

20. (d) There are 8 rectangles and 9 circles in the picture.

21. (a) All carrots are vegetables. All vegetables are food.

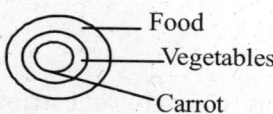

(22 - 25):

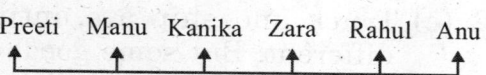

22. (c) Anu is sitting right to the Rahul.

23. (b) Kanika and Zara are sitting in the middle in the row.

24. (b) Kanika sitting second to the left of Rahul is correct statement.

25. (a) Manu is sitting immediate left of Kanika.

26. (a) All pigeons are birds. But, dogs are entirely different.

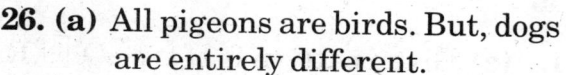

27. (a)

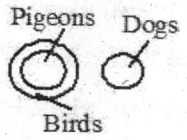

28. (c) Option (c) is correct answer.

29. (c)

30. (d) 1 litre = 1000 ml
4 litre = 4 × 1000 = 4000 ml
and 250 + 250 = 500 ml
Therefore, total volume of water in six container
= 4000 + 500 = 4500 ml

MOCK TEST-2

ANSWERS KEY

1.	(c)	7.	(c)	13.	(a)	19.	(b)	25.	(b)
2.	(a)	8.	(a)	14.	(a)	20.	(d)	26.	(c)
3.	(d)	9.	(b)	15.	(d)	21.	(c)	27.	(b)
4.	(a)	10.	(b)	16.	(b)	22.	(c)	28.	(a)
5.	(a)	11.	(b)	17.	(c)	23.	(c)	29.	(d)
6.	(a)	12.	(a)	18.	(c)	24.	(b)	30.	(c)

46

Hints & Explanations

1. (c) Given pattern is of type Q [P] R
   Pattern followed, P = Q × R
   i.e., 123 × 7 = 861 ; 51 × 7 = 357;
   51 × 9 = 459 ; 9 × 102 = 918

2. (a) Word formed is FRUIT, i.e., arrangement of numbers should be 4, 2, 5, 3, 1.

3. (d) Letter E in the word NOSE is not in the given word.

4. (a)

5. (a) Fisherman is related to fish and fish is called snake.

6. (a)
7. (c)
8. (a)

9. (b)
   Mirror

10. (b)

    B2E5R9 | 9R5E2B
    Mirror

11. (b)
12. (a)
13. (a)
14. (a)
15. (d) If second day is Friday, then next Friday will be after 7 days from Friday.
    $2^{nd}, 9^{th}, 16^{th}, 23^{rd}, 30^{th}$ are dates on which Friday occurs.

16. (b) 2nd Sunday of July 20XX is on 13th. Garima will celebrate her birthday on 14th July 20XX.

17. (c) In first figure of left pair, inner figure becomes the outer figure, middle becomes inner, and outer becomes the middle figure of second figure.

18. (c) Numbers in (a), (b) and (d) are the multiples of 2 or even numbers.

19. (b)

20. (d)

21. (c) Option (c) is correct answer.

22. (c) Truck and ship are entirely different. But some goods are carried by some trucks and some goods are carried by some ships.

    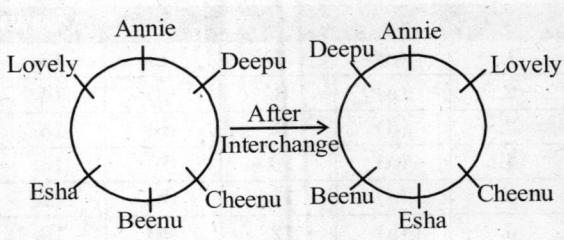

23. (c)

24. (b) There are 7 triangles in the figure.

(Sol. 25 - 29) :

Hints & Explanations

25. (b) Annie will be sitting to the left of Deepu.

26. (c) Esha will be sitting to the left of Cheenu.

27. (b) Esha will be sitting to the opposite to the Annie.

28. (a) Cheenu and Annie are the neighbours of Lovely.

29. (d) Annie is sitting to the right of lovely.

30. (c)

MOCK TEST-3

ANSWERS KEY

1.	(b)	6.	(a)	11.	(b)	16.	(a)	21.	(a)
2.	(a)	7.	(b)	12.	(a)	17.	(d)	22.	(d)
3.	(a)	8.	(c)	13.	(a)	18.	(c)	23.	(d)
4.	(d)	9.	(a)	14.	(b)	19.	(c)	24.	(a)
5.	(d)	10.	(d)	15.	(b)	20.	(d)	25.	(d)

1. (b) 2 × 2 = 4, 4 × 2 = 8, 8 × 2 = 16, 16 × 2 = 32, 32 × 2 = 64, 64 × 2 = 128

2. (a) Word formed is S T A R, which gives us light.

3. (a) All the letters of the word MASTER are in given word.

or

L, I & S letters of the words in options (b), (c) and (d) are not in the given word.

4. (d) Deer lives in forest and forest is called building.

5. (d)

6. (a) New arrangement will be P Q R S T U V W

7. (b)

8. (c)
| Komal |
| Megha |
| Sapna |
| Riya |
| Kriti |

9. (a)

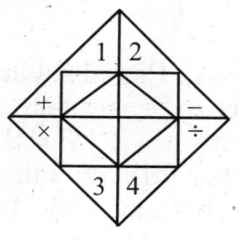 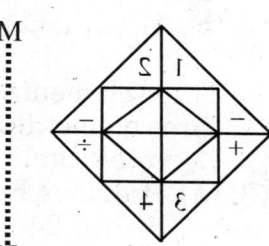

Hints & Explanations

10. (d)

11. (b)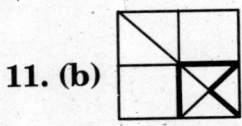

12. (a)

13. (a)
She will facing north.

14. (b)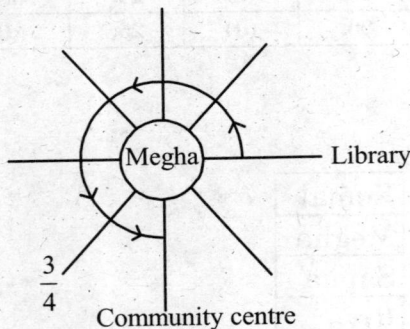

15. (b) Pencil : (P_1, P_2, P_3) and Eraser : (E_1, E_2, E_3)
Possible combinations : (P_1, E_1), (P_1, E_2), (P_1, E_3), (P_2, E_1), (P_2, E_2), (P_2, E_3), (P_3, E_1), (P_3, E_2), (P_3, E_3).
or
Three elements are in Pencil set and three elements are in eraser set.
∴ total combination = 3 × 3 = 9

16. (a) Previous Friday falls on 7 days before 24th February, i.e., 17th February.

17. (d) Figures (a), (b) and (c) are symmetrical along MN.

18. (c) Figure (i) and (iii) are formed by only curved lines and fig (ii) and fig (iv) are formed by only straight lines.

19. (c) There are 10 handshakes that took place.

20. (d) There are 4 horizontal lines in the adjoining figure.

(Sol. 21-23) : The arrangement is as follows :

	Hockey	Volleyball	Baseball	Cricket	Football
Rohit	√	√	√	×	×
Kapil	√	√	×	√	×
Sagar	√	×	√	×	√
Gaurav	×	√	√	√	√
Mohit	×	×	√	×	√

21. (a) Kapil is good in Cricket, Volleyball and Hockey.

22. (d) Gaurav is good in Football, Volleyball, Baseball and Cricket.

23. (d) Rohit is good in Hockey and Baseball.

24. (a) Elephants and Wolves bear no relationship to each other. But, both of them are animals.

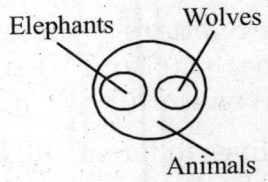

25. (d) Option (d) is correct answer.

Hints & Explanations

MOCK TEST-4

ANSWERS KEY

1.	(a)	6.	(a)	11.	(b)	16.	(c)	21.	(c)
2.	(c)	7.	(c)	12.	(a)	17.	(a)	22.	(d)
3.	(c)	8.	(b)	13.	(d)	18.	(d)	23.	(b)
4.	(b)	9.	(c)	14.	(b)	19.	(a)	24.	(c)
5.	(c)	10.	(d)	15.	(a)	20.	(b)	25.	(c)

1. **(a)** Number of circles in pattern 1 = 4,
   Number of circles in pattern 2 = 7
   Number of circles in pattern 3 = 10
   Therefore, the pattern is +3

2. **(c)** Word formed is W A T E R and is used for drinking.

3. **(c)** S and T letters of the words in options (a), (b) and (d) are not in the given word.

4. **(b)** ☐ has exactly four lines of symmetry and ☐ means ◯.

5. **(c)** Prime factors of 45 are 3, 5 and 5 means 7.

6. **(a)**

7. **(c)**

8. **(b)**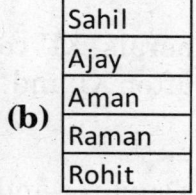

9. **(c)**

10. **(d)**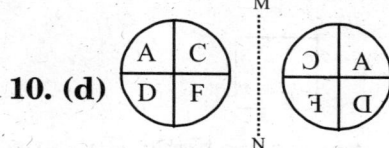

11. **(b)**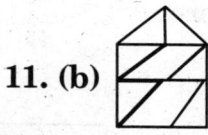

12. **(a)**

13. **(d)**

14. **(b)**

15. **(a)** Possible combinations :
    3   4 = 12

16. **(c)**

Hints & Explanations

June 20XX						
S	M	T	W	Th	F	S
	1	2	3	4	5	6
7	8	9	10	11	12	13
14	15	16	17	18	19	20
21	22	23	24	25	26	27
28	29	30				

Latika will practice for 15 days.

17. (a) Figure (iii) is the right rotated part of figure (i).

18. (d) Numbers in (a), (b) and (c) are all prime numbers.

19. (a) Option (a) is correct answer.

20. (b) All sparrows are birds. But, mice are entirely different.

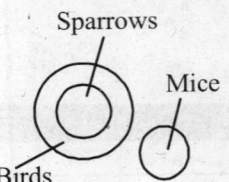

21. (c)

22. (d) There are 10 squares in the figure.

(Sol. 23-24): The arrangement of five houses is as following:

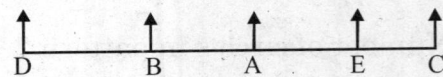

23. (b) A is in the middle of the row.

24. (c) E sits immediate right of A.

25. (c) Option (c) is correct answer.

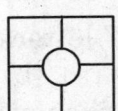

MOCK TEST-5

ANSWERS KEY

1.	(b)	6.	(a)	11.	(b)	16.	(c)	21.	(c)
2.	(d)	7.	(b)	12.	(a)	17.	(a)	22.	(c)
3.	(b)	8.	(a)	13.	(d)	18.	(b)	23.	(a)
4.	(b)	9.	(c)	14.	(a)	19.	(a)	24.	(b)
5.	(c)	10.	(a)	15.	(d)	20.	(d)	25.	(d)

1. (b) Series followed :

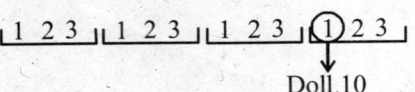
Doll 10

2. (d) Given Letters : C, E, O, Q

3. (b) Possible words : URN, RUN

4. (b) In roman numerals, XII comes immediately after XI and XIII means C.

5. (c) ⬛ formed by squares and △

means ▯.

Hints & Explanations

6. (a)
7. (b) New arrangement

   A 3 Q R ⑥ W X P T U I 4 E S ① V Y Z

8. (a)

   A ✗ Q R ✗ W X P T U I ✗ E S ✗ V Y Z

9. (c)

10. (a)

11. (b)

12. (a)
13. (d)
14. (a) Priya remembers the dates are 19 and 20 but her father remembers date is an odd number, i.e., 19th March.
15. (d)
16. (c)
17. (a) Figure (iii) is the mirror image of figure (i).

(Sol. 18-19):

T-shirt	Star	Flower	Flag	Polka Dot
Avika	×	×	√	×
Liya	×	√	×	×
Bulbul	√	×	×	×
Janvi	×	×	×	√

18. (b) Avika has flag printed T-shirt.
19. (a) Bulbul has star printed T-shirt.
20. (d) There are 12 triangles in the figure.
21. (c) Here, 1 hr = 60 mins

    So, 60 mins + 30 mins = 90 mins

    Therefore, 90/9 = 10 mins

    Hence, number of minutes she took to solve one problem is 10.
22. (c) Option (c) is correct answer.

23. (a) Some boys are students. Some students are athletes. Some boys are athletes. So, the given items are partly related to each other.

    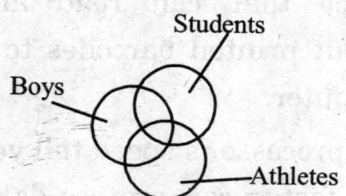

24. (b) 12 possible combinations can be made.
25. (d) There are 16 sides.

CYBER

MOCK TEST 1

ANSWER KEY

1.	(a)	6.	(b)	11.	(d)	16.	(d)	21.	(d)
2.	(c)	7.	(a)	12.	(d)	17.	(c)	22.	(a)
3.	(b)	8.	(a)	13.	(a)	18.	(a)	23.	(c)
4.	(a)	9.	(a)	14.	(a)	19.	(d)	24.	(a)
5.	(d)	10.	(a)	15.	(a)	20.	(a)	25.	(d)

1. **(a)** The Zip drive is a medium-to-high-capacity (at the time of its release) removable floppy disk storage system that was introduced by Iomega in late 1994. Originally, Zip disks were launched with capacities of 100 MB, but later versions increased this to first 250 MB and then 750 MB.

2. **(c)** A barcode reader (or barcode scanner) is an electronic device that can read and output printed barcodes to a computer.

4. **(a)** The processor's speed tell you how fast it can process data. And RAM determines how much instructions a computer can hold before going to the processor.

5. **(d)** Abacus was the first mechanical calculator. It is used to perform the basic operations of arithmetic.

6. **(b)** Fifth Generation of computer is still under development.

7. **(a)** Piece of hardware EIDE cables connect to is hard disk.

8. **(a)** Any device connected to a computer but not a part of it is called peripheral hardware device.

9. **(a)** The full form of CMOS is Complementary metal–oxide–semiconductor.

10. **(a)** A set of instruction for your computer is correct about the software program.

13. **(a)** While working with MS-Paint, text tool is used to add name to your drawing.

Hints & Explanations

14. (a) Skew can create an effect that can be used in making an illusion of 3D perspective.

17. (c) www.hotmail.com is the correct internet address.

18. (a) ARPANET was the name of the first network.

19. (d) Easy sharing of internet connects computers, transfer of data from one computer to another and sharing printers and other devices among connected computers are correct about the networking.

20. (a) Local Area Network (LAN) is computer network that interconnects computers within a limited area such as a residence, school, and laboratory.

21. (d) In MS-Word 2010, red and green colour wavy line under a word indicates a spelling or grammar mistake.

22. (a) Microsoft Word 2010 is a word processing software.

24. (a) Windows is an operating system.

MOCK TEST 2

ANSWER KEY

1.	(d)	6.	(b)	11.	(d)	16.	(a)	21.	(a)
2.	(c)	7.	(a)	12.	(b)	17.	(d)	22.	(b)
3.	(a)	8.	(a)	13.	(a)	18.	(c)	23.	(c)
4.	(a)	9.	(a)	14.	(c)	19.	(a)	24.	(c)
5.	(b)	10.	(d)	15.	(d)	20.	(c)	25.	(c)

2. (c) A hand-held scanner is any scanner that is held in the hand of the user during operation.

8. (a) Modern computer, Motherboards have a backup battery to run the realtime clock circuit and retain configuration memory while the system is turned off.

This is offen called the CMOS battery or BIOS battary.

54

13. **(a)** Colour 1, Colour 2 boxes are used to
   1. Select the Foreground colour, click the Colour 1 box, and select your desired colour from the colour palette to the right.
   2. Select the Background colour, click the Colour 2 box, and

Hints & Explanations

select your desired colour from the colour palette to the right.

15. **(d)** Only option (d) because that can be used to bring a zoomed in or a zoomed out image to its original size.

MOCK TEST 3

ANSWER KEY

1.	(a)	6.	(b)	11.	(d)	16.	(d)	21.	(c)
2.	(a)	7.	(d)	12.	(d)	17.	(a)	22.	(a)
3.	(d)	8.	(a)	13.	(d)	18.	(c)	23.	(a)
4.	(a)	9.	(b)	14.	(b)	19.	(b)	24.	(b)
5.	(d)	10.	(c)	15.	(d)	20.	(a)	25.	(d)

1. **(a)** It is a mouse-like input device, where you roll a ball on the top of the device to move the cursor on the screen.

13. **(d)** STP (Shielded Twisted pair) and UTP (Unshielded Twisted Pair) are the type of twisted pair cable, which are mostly used in all types of network.

14. **(b)** NIC is the Network interface card which is used to connect the computer to the network.

18. **(c)** Option (c) tool is used to select all portions of the image rather then selecting the particular part of the image.

21. **(c)** Operating systems control the computer hardware and act as an interface with application programs. And utility software helps to manage, maintain and control computer resources. Examples of utility softwares are antivirus software, backup software.

22. **(a)** In computing, firmware is a computer program that is "embedded" in a hardware device and is an essential part of the hardware. It is sometimes called embedded software. An example is a microcontroller.